so you want to
dance on
broadway?

so you want to
dance on
broadway?

Insight and Advice from the Pros Who Know

Tina Paul

Foreword by Tommy Tune

HEINEMANN
Portsmouth, NH

Heinemann
A division of Reed Elsevier Inc.
361 Hanover Street
Portsmouth, NH 03801–3912
www.heinemanndrama.com

Offices and agents throughout the world

© 2003 by Tina Paul

Library of Congress Cataloging-in-Publication Data
Paul, Tina.
    So you want to dance on Broadway? : insight and advice from the pros
who know / Tina Paul.
        p.   cm.
    ISBN 0-325-00536-2 (pbk. : alk. paper)
    1. Dance—Vocational guidance.   I. Title.
GV1597 .P38 2003
793.3'023—dc21

                                                    2002153290

Editor: Lisa Barnett
Production: Lynne Reed
Cover design: Night & Day Design
Typesetter: Kim Arney Mulcahy
Manufacturing: Steve Bernier

Printed in the United States of America on acid-free paper
07   06   05   04   03   DA   1   2   3   4   5

This book is dedicated

To my mom and dad, who tolerated my
claiming the playroom to enact every part in *My Fair
Lady* when I was six . . .

To my brothers and sister, who goaded me to impersonate Elvis Presley when I was young enough to be shameless . . .

To my husband and son, who lovingly tiptoed through
the house while I wrote this book . . .

To the fourteen contributors to this book, who trusted
me with their stories . . .

And to all the dancers—the artistic athletes of Broadway—who now or someday will feel the thrill of the
backstage call, "Places, please."

Contents

Foreword

5-6-7-8-Read

I've nicknamed this insightful volume *The Gypsy Handbook*. Others may call it *The Broadway Performer's Survival Manual* or even *The Divine Secrets of the Showbiz Dancerhood*. It's *A Chorus Line* how-to in literary form. Whatever we dub it, and we will, it's so incredibly valuable that I'm jealous it didn't exist when I first hit New York. Straight up from Texas, I was seeking a chorus job on the Great White Way. This detailed book would have alleviated a lot of my trepidations. I'm so glad that it exists today for you.

Tina Paul has done an excellent job assembling thoughts, advice, information, inside dope, intimate revelations, while along the way dispelling myths, and finally, delivering inspiration from the cross section of working professionals that she's interviewed. Their words, mixed with her own sound advice, make for an incomparable recipe. The emerging theme seems to be "You are not alone," and that's comforting.

So you want to dance on Broadway. Well, good fortune has already come your way; you've picked up this book! It will answer your questions and will surely prepare you for most situations to come. I thoroughly recommend it to you. It's a really, really honest assessment of the Broadway scene by those who are living it. And did I mention that it's hilarious?

So, listen up, here's your choreography: 5-6-7-8-Read.

Tommy Tune

NEW YORK CITY

so you want to

dance on
broadway?

CHAPTER ONE

What's the Big Deal?

So you want to dance on Broadway. Why? What is the allure of a career where you have to compete with thousands of other people for a job, where you have no guarantees that if you get a job it will last, and you will never be taken seriously by mortgage brokers? Do you really want to study for more years than a physician, live in a fifth-floor walk-up with too many roommates, and know that as good as you are you'll always have to struggle to be better? Dance on Broadway. Why?

JIM BORSTELMANN: I didn't choose this career, it chose me. I love to perform. In the neighborhood we would dance every night under the streetlight. Then I saw *West Side Story* and I had to be one of those gang members. They were real guys and they were so fluid and could leap and jump and sing and dance and tell a story through dance. Dance? Gotta do it. It's fun. It's what I was put on this earth to do. I'm convinced of that. There's nothing else I want to do. Bottom line.

GRACIELA DANIELE: I remember the first day I went into dance class as if it was yesterday. The studio had mirrors on both sides. When I came in and looked in the mirror, what I saw in the reflection was space. Infinity. I wanted to run through that space. Conquer it. It was freedom. After years of ballet, what later inspired me to come to Broadway was the opportunity of working with great directors, choreographers, designers, composers, and lyricists. It is the advantage of working on Broadway.

TOMMY TUNE: Although I had taken dance lessons since I was five, I didn't know what a Broadway musical was. Living way down in Texas, we didn't have road shows and we didn't have television. But in high school a friend took me to see a dress rehearsal of *The King and I* at a local community theatre. Sitting in the dark, I saw the dancing, and then there was talking—a story—and then there was singing to express what was more than just talking. It was so beautiful and so touching and so magical, it wrecked me. I kept asking my friend, "What is this?" and she said, *"The King and I."* I said, "Well, I know what it's called, but what is it? This isn't a play because I've seen a play. What is this?" She said, "This is what they do on Broadway. This is a Broadway musical." Well, that was it for me. It was like a sea-change in my life, an about-face, because this Broadway thing wasn't just dancing anymore. It all came together for me.

MAMIE DUNCAN-GIBBS: Dancing kind of snuck into my life. It was not allowed in my house. My mother was very religious and dancing was considered a sin—girls with boas dancing on bars and straddling men's laps. So for me, I was like, "Get me out of here!" When I was eleven I convinced my mother to let me take gymnastics with the minister's daughter, telling her it was just exercise. My class only lasted an hour, but I'd stay all day watching the other dancers so I wouldn't have to wash the woodwork and iron clothes at home. It's ironic that I became a Broadway dancer because it was such a struggle—no support, no money, playing catch-up on dance technique. But I knew I had to try to get to Broadway. How do you go through life not trying? By forever wondering, "What if?" I wouldn't, couldn't do anything else but dance. It's freedom.

LUIS PEREZ: Although I was a principal with the Joffrey Ballet, I started out as a fan of Gene Kelly. To see him dance, sing, act, and get the girl— that's what I wanted to do. I bought cast albums of Broadway shows and would read the librettos from the library. I prayed nightly for God to let me dance. Ballet was my in-road, but the allure of Broadway always stayed with me—the complete picture of the three disciplines: the fun of telling stories, bursting into song, and the freedom of flying through space.

JULIO MONGE: I always had my eye on Broadway. My mother has my old eighth-grade notebooks. I would write, "Julio Monge—Broadway!" Dance is my foundation—I love it. When I dance I get transported, and not just from my hometown in Puerto Rico to Broadway. I am obsessed. Dancers are such different creatures yet everybody identifies with our art. The audience sees a beautiful female dancer in a show and drools over her, not because of the sexuality, but because of the power and strength that is behind it. Watch Gene Kelly or Baryshnikov—their approach, masculinity, energy. Dancers are passionate, hard-working, open, dedicated to their craft. We sweat and cut to the chase. When we combine all of that with telling a story on a Broadway stage, we are members of a very special breed.

CHITA RIVERA: When I step on a Broadway stage, I like it. It's a positive place, almost religious. That wonderful stage space holds such fascination, such freedom, such a variety of steps, music, and rhythm left by others. I love dancing for people, seeing what happens to them whether I'm silly or serious or whatever. Dance is something inside of me that needs to come out all the time. Someone once painted a caricature of me where, from every angle of me, there were arrows. I recognized it as energy wanting to touch space because dancers know that motion doesn't stop at the ends of your fingers. Dance is electricity, color, heat, temperature, and as dancers I believe we have the opportunity to be closer to the universe than anybody.

DAVID WARREN-GIBSON: Dance feeds my spirit. I always think of dance like food—I'll starve if I don't have it, whether I'm in a room alone where no one can see me or onstage. When I've gone away from dance for a few days, I'm hungry but literal food won't do it. Nothing does. I've got to dance. I've got to dance to the music. And then I feel full again. You know when you actually float on a pirouette? You don't weigh anything, you don't or can't stop. The feeling? If heaven exists, that must be what it is.

BEBE NEUWIRTH: When I was born the doctor pulled me from my mother and said, "She's a dancer." At four I saw *The Nutcracker* and was so overwhelmingly drawn to the space, the sound, the freedom, and the vision of dance, I experienced an "Ah! That's who I am. That's what I am. That's what I do." Ballet was my world, my love, but the heartbreak was that while I was a terrific performer, I didn't have that bizarre thing, that technical perfection, to be a great ballerina. Luckily I saw *Pippin* when I was thirteen and Fosse's choreography resonated with me as deeply as ballet. I internally shifted my focus and thought, "I'm going to dance on Broadway. I'm going to do that guy's choreography." I was on another tangent and my path was clear.

MICHAEL KUBALA: Coming from a small town and doing regional theatre, my ultimate goal was to eventually move on and try to make a living on Broadway. In regional theatre I got the encouragement to explore talents I didn't even know I had, but you do shows that are already established. I knew that to be an original cast member in a Broadway show meant that you would be part of the creation—the definition of a character that future performers in regional theatre would someday emulate. Achieving that level of creativity, that freedom, would be a dream come true.

JOANN M. HUNTER: My father was completely against me dancing. He wanted me to be a lawyer, to make something of myself. He was also an alcoholic, so the worse the drinking got, the worse dancing became something stupid and useless to him. But in the summer before my senior year of high school, I came to New York on a scholarship with Chuck Kelly and knew that Broadway was where I wanted to be. It wasn't a logical choice, but more like an epiphany. I called home and told my mom I wasn't going back to finish high school. We tried for an earlier graduation since I had met my high school requirements, but the school wouldn't allow it, so I left. I had to. Performing is what I love. If a person had the opportunity to do something extraordinary like living on Mars, that's what performing on Broadway feels like to me.

EUGENE FLEMING: My sister and I were the first African Americans in an all-white dancing school back in the late '60s. Luckily the teachers were cool, though I did wonder why my mother always sat in the car when she dropped us off. Basically the teachers taught off phonograph records and would give us combinations they had written down. So coming from this small dancing school in Virginia, I didn't know that Broadway existed. It never entered my mind that theatre could be a career. When I went to the North Carolina School of the Arts and the School of American Ballet, my eyes opened to other things going on, but dancing was still just something fun to do. At the same time, I didn't know what else

I wanted to be. So I just did Broadway and it did me and it kept going until a life happened. What I have found out is that the stage is where I shine; this is what I am here to do. I'm a showman. When I perform, I go into orbit.

CAITLIN CARTER: My world was all ballet, ballet, ballet from the time I was seven through my teenage years, but musical theatre opened a whole new element to me. The acting, the music—I have a blast. Although there's a lot of great theatre around the country, Broadway was my goal. I love the pressure, the hype, and being able to earn enough money to make a living.

ROBERT MONTANO: I was a professional racehorse jockey when I was sixteen and didn't start dancing until I was twenty. It killed me to leave racing because that was all I ever wanted to do. I loved the speed, danger, excitement, the thunder, and even the crowd heckling me when I lost. But I was growing every minute and time was running out. I struggled to keep my weight down, but I literally outgrew the Sport of Kings. My world was shattered. That's when I found dance. My sister convinced me to audition for Adelphi University where I was offered a scholarship. Even though I knew nothing of ballet and modern, I eventually developed a passion for it. But after my first month I told them that this modern thing was cool but I wanted to dance that—I didn't know what to call it—but it was fast and alone. The teacher laughed and said, "That's jazz. You have to go into the city for that." So I went into Manhattan and found jazz. And Broadway. And my future.

My first inkling that I would make dance my career came onstage at twelve years old. I realized that before or after my recital number, people could yell at me, but for those moments onstage I was untouchable. Free. Although I then immersed myself in pure dance for a number of years, Broadway was my ultimate goal. Where else is there such an artistic combination of dancing, singing, and acting for musical theatre? Although there are astounding developmental theatres, Broadway is still considered the hub—the legend—the best. I could imagine no better career where hard work would never seem like work, where the opportunity to portray different characters is limitless, and where I could earn a decent salary to boot.

Since devoting myself to Broadway, I have enjoyed a long career and many an opening night. What an incomparable wonder that is! With every show artists come together to fill the landscape of the stage with their dreams, and the opening night is the culmination of their visions. Whether the show is a winner or a rotter, for that one night everyone celebrates the hard work, the achievement, and the miracle of creating an evening of magic where there was no magic before. From the parade of the gypsy robe before the show until the reviews hit the newsstand, you ride in a whirlwind of congratulations, gifts, roses, applause, and slammin' parties. This is no bronze statuette, certificate of merit, or gold watch for a job well done. This is energy and illusion joining together to give you a slap on the back for helping the dream come true. Such nights are hard to find in a career with a time clock. On Broadway, they are a given.

So you want to dance on Broadway? Good for you. As hard as it may be to get there, you will join a group of talented, determined people who thrive off the freedom that comes with extraordinary discipline. You will smell the mingled makeup on your dressing-room towel and hear the roar of the crowd on your opening night bow, guaranteed. You will be singled out by the richest and the poorest, most of whom would kill to be in your shoes for just one minute. It is not safe. It is not careful. It is sweat-soaked, tear-ridden, exhilarating bliss.

The question is how to do it.

CHAPTER TWO

You Want to What?!

Robert Joffrey used to say, "There are three things that make a good dancer: determination, a good teacher, and talent."

— Luis Perez

Although Mr. Joffrey was from the ballet world, his definition is right on the money. Ballet dancer, Broadway dancer—the style doesn't matter. The key words are *good dancer,* and a good dancer you must be to meet the demands of Broadway. Before vying for a spot on the Broadway stage, it is wise to assess your current talents and teachers in order to guarantee that you are as prepared as possible. Through Chapters 2, 3, and 4 we will deal with the necessary elements cited by Mr. Joffrey—determination, teachers, and the talents you must develop to become a triple threat. The first encompasses love of craft, guts, and self-awareness.

Dance 'Til You Drop

Many things in life can be faked. A synthesizer can simulate an orchestra, computer imaging can populate a film with some pretty nasty dinosaurs, and microwaveable food can make you seem like a fairly decent cook. But dance is the flesh-and-blood you, and it cannot be fabricated or fast-forwarded for instant results. This is the beauty of it, but it is a concept that is sometimes difficult to endure in today's high-speed world of "I want it yesterday." No dancer, anywhere, is perfect. You must not only face this reality, but also thrive on it. The inspiring challenge is to never settle for less, and to enjoy working on the thousandth plié as much as the first. A dancer may luckily land one show without advanced technique, but only determination and dedication to your craft will build a career.

Navigating Family, Friends, and Foes

Most dancers who set their sights on Broadway do it from high school through college age. This means that you are usually living with or are financially supported by your parents and you go to a normal school with normal friends. In other words, there are rules, opinions, and peer pressure that may make your dream of dancing on Broadway seem worse than digging up your dead grandmother and serving her for dinner. In some cases, kids are exposed to show business because their parents make their living on Broadway as performers, directors, choreographers, and so on. However, this is not the norm. Most Broadway dancers come from families whose involvement in theatre is watching the first hour of the Macy's Thanksgiving Day Parade. As a result, you may not get encouragement or credit for the hours, months, years it takes to gain the expertise to maintain a career on Broadway. This lack of credit can be a downer, especially when you are asked, "When are you going to get a real job?" If any odds are stacked against you, it is only your determination that will lead you on the road to success.

TOMMY TUNE: I was hell-bent to dance and come hell or high water, that's what I was going to do. I had choreographed quite a lot in high school and everybody thought I should be a choreographer. But after college I got realistic. I knew from reading about people like Jerome Robbins and Peter Gennaro and all those choreographers listed on show albums that they were dancers first before they moved into choreographing. So I thought, "Okay, that's what I gotta do. I'm going to go to New York and get into the chorus of a Broadway show. I'll start at ground level and see how it goes." I didn't realize what a hard dream that was, being this tall. But I wouldn't listen to anyone who told me I was too tall because that's what I had to do. That's how it was going to work for me. I was going to get to Broadway. And, bang! I came to New York and the first day I had an audition for a touring company of *Irma La Douce* and I got the job. Even though it was a tour, my dream to dance in the chorus of a Broadway show had come true.

JULIO MONGE: The only one who could have stood in my way was my father but he totally took off when I was twelve years old. He was a heavy-duty truck driver. Hard worker, but he drank a lot and liked a lot of women. He was not a monster, but he was not a good leader in the house. By my nature I just sort of took charge of my family while he became a figure in silhouette. I could work around him. My mother was fine with my performing all along. I was such a good student and she trusted me. I earned that trust where there was no doubt in her head that whatever I was pursuing, it was going to be fine.

MICHAEL KUBALA: My mother thought I had a natural ability so she had no problem with my dancing, but toward the end of high school we weren't getting along that well because of my involvement in theatre. I was starting to stay out late and she had her own life, going away on weekends. I was having growing pains, I was my own caretaker, and I didn't want to be anyone's son anymore.

EUGENE FLEMING: I led a very Jekyll and Hyde life. At night I'd go to dance school, this happy, smiley guy, but during my daytime hours at high school, I was cool—playing sports, hitting on the girls, that sort of thing. I wouldn't let anyone know I danced. Some of the guys knew I tap danced and called me Shirley Temple or Bojangles, but because I was one of the cool guys, they wouldn't jump on me too much. Then I did *The Nutcracker* and there was a picture of me on the front page of the entertainment paper doing a jump split in the Russian number. The basketball coach brought it to practice. That was hard. I got razzed by the guys, but the weird thing about it was the coach made it work. He said, "That's my Bubba,"—Bubba was my nickname—"He can do all those kind of moves with the ball that none of you guys can do because he dances. He floats. Now you can razz him on it, but . . ." I think he could really see that I had something else going on that was a little bit beyond all the normal players.

<u>Mamie Duncan-Gibbs:</u> When I auditioned for Juilliard I had good grades but not enough technique so I didn't get in. My mother said, "See, I told you it's not for you to dance." I even had a school counselor say, "Well, you're not supposed to dance so that's why you didn't get into the school." I remember thinking, "How dare you destroy my dream?" and then, "Okay, so I didn't get into Juilliard. I'll figure out another way." I had already figured out how to take what classes I could up until then for no money. I realized that people aren't necessarily going to agree with me or care. It made me put up a little wall to do what I needed to do for me because I loved it.

Understandably, choosing Broadway as a career might send your parents over the edge. They want only the best life for you—safe, secure, loving. They are right. They have been around the block raising you, knowing what it takes to make a buck, and knowing that the world can be a KO to the kisser. It is not fair to expect them to dance a fandango over your decision. It is up to you alone to follow your dream. I do believe it is easier for women to garner acceptance. It may be disappointing to your parents that you won't be the next Madame Curie, but if dancing on Broadway doesn't work out, there's a safeguard in the back of everyone's mind: heck, you can always get married! You might even snag a rich producer-type with a fat cigar and ringside seats at Madison Square Garden.

But for men we're talking about entering a profession where the pay is sporadic, work can evaporate with a torn hamstring, and supporting a family is just plain scary. And then—dare I say it? People may tag you as a sissy. I have never, ever heard anyone say to a woman, "Dancing makes you a lesbian," but there is no doubt that by dancing, you will be handing any jackass who has ever made love to a carburetor enough ammunition to wound the most macho of men. An extreme amount of determination comes into play here to resist calling it quits because of a label.

The Whole Gay Question

The taunting that the guys, gay and straight, can experience is tough.

<u>Julio Monge:</u> By the town's standards if you sang, danced, were in the theatre, the choir, anything that seemed a little poetic, you were stamped as gay. If they saw you in a leotard, they'd freak out.

What I find so ridiculous is the notion that dance can *make* you turn gay. Let's be logical. Sexual preference is not picked up like poison ivy. Dance can no more make you gay than being in the Marines can make you straight. It's such rubbish. There are gay people in theatre, and people who swing both ways, and there are many straight people, too. You have a right to your proclivity. But straight or gay, you have to live through the derision of those who question that right. Unfortunately, from grammar school on, kids start using words like "homo." The only exposure they've had to anything "homo" is homogenized milk, but these early sexual innuendos tend to blossom into full-grown prejudice in adults. Dancers are easy targets. Once you get to New York City, it will be easier for you to live as you choose, but in the meantime, you have to find a way to bring them around or ignore them—whatever it takes to survive the jabs.

MICHAEL KUBALA: When I went to tap class I would walk with my shoes in a paper bag because I didn't want anybody to know what they were. I'd crinkle the bag up under my armpits and look around the corner to make sure nobody saw me going into the studio. I kind of kept my dancing closeted until I got into community theatre.

TOMMY TUNE: It wasn't until junior high school that the sissy thing came up. I was coming out of the school auditorium with my tap shoes because I had been rehearsing for a show, and these kind of hoods called me a queer. I didn't know what it meant so the next day in school I went to the library to look it up. They had one of those giant dictionaries that were real thick up on a stand. So I stepped up and flipped to the Q's. I got to where *queer* was and there was a hole in the paper. So many people had looked it up, there was a hole! So I skipped down to *queerer*, thinking that that would be close enough. The definition was "queerer: one who queers." I still didn't know! But you know what? There's always that thing that makes it hard for guys to be dancers. But if you have to dance, you can't be bothered by what you are going to be called. Dance is a calling, like taking a vow or something. If God is calling you, you're going to become a priest or a nun. Dance was calling me and I had to be a dancer.

LUIS PEREZ: There were some people who made fun of me, but they weren't really my friends. I didn't care. I was too busy doing what I wanted to do. I realized that those who are prejudiced negate an entire part of life. Everything in life is a dance. Why do you think they put music behind the NFL playbacks as the players run, jump, and catch the ball in slow motion? Why do people watch MTV and enjoy the dancing? From earliest man there has been movement to music; they are firmly combined. It is a part of who we are.

JIM BORSTELMANN: No matter how many shows we did on the street or in the community theatre, only two of my friends actually took formal dance classes. My neighbor across the street took class at the June Claire School of Dance. We'd kid him about it, but not too much because we were all so close—like cousins. How much are you going to pick on your blood? Besides, he had a built-in pool in his backyard, so—politics.

JULIO MONGE: I got ribbed in school but I was a very popular student. I got all A's, I was the president of my class. I totally knew how to manipulate them. I wasn't intimidated. It was hurtful at times but I had a good support system. There was a group of us who stuck together from seventh to eleventh grade, the crucial years of being a teenager. All of us were equally good students, we all loved singing and dancing, and we put on programs together. The school loved us. They sort of respected us.

ROBERT MONTANO: At the racetrack, forget it. There was no such thing as homosexuality or it wasn't spoken of if there was. It was an encapsulated world. Back then, the guys I hung with just drank, gambled, and fucked. You started young and grew up quick—Bingo! Instant man! God forbid I told these guys I was going to college for a degree in dance. This one ballbuster happened to find out and that was the end of me. He endlessly cracked my nuts and called me "Twinkle Toes" and other shit that you can only imagine. He always shouted, "Bobby-boy, the star of nothing. Stage or screen, nothing!" He is still galloping horses today, but with a different attitude. When I visit Belmont these days he now says, "Bobby-boy, we're proud of you, you prick. You did the right thing. You moved on and made it."

Whether you are straight or gay, you have the freedom to express it in any way you choose, except by doing such unprofessional things as copping a feel in the dressing room or making lewd comments during class. (I have often had to tolerate numskulls offering, "I can help you with your turnout," or remarking, "Your legs would make a great necklace." This type of disrespectful behavior should be aimed at neither woman nor man.) However, as a male dancer, your technique and persona should not unalterably reflect your sexual preference. The dancing in most Broadway shows is rooted in conventional characterization. Usually girls are girls, and boys are boys. Certainly there are shows that portray different lifestyles, but being limited to performing in *La Cage Aux Folles* or *Victor, Victoria* does not a career make. Even at that, the stronger dancer, gay or straight, will get the job as long as he looks good in stockings. So many times I have seen wonderfully trained dancers not get jobs because they didn't look "male enough" when they danced. It's the reality of the business. So have a blast in your everyday life, but work like a dog in class to be the best male dancer you can be. Your talent and strength will then be irrefutable.

Body Beautiful or Betrayal

Nature blesses each of us with many physical attributes when we are born, but often we feel as if we were skipped over when the best ones were doled out. Why does one person get the high arch and another the long legs? Why can one dancer eat junk food and not gain an ounce while another constantly fights a weight war no matter the stringent diet? Tall, short, big nose, button nose, thick hair, bald spots—every inch of our bodies is a jigsaw piece that seldom combines into a self-satisfying puzzle. Some things you can change with hard work and determination, others through plastic surgery and implants, and others will accompany you to your grave. The question is to what extent you go, wisely or not, to transform your body.

Of utmost importance is to recognize that as a dancer your body is your instrument. The more it is a well-oiled, healthy, lean mean fighting machine, the better your chances are of excelling in your technique and presenting an attractive image. As a Broadway dancer, especially for women, you do not need to be unhealthily thin. Rather, your body should have no excess fat, like the kind that jiggles or seems to disappear only when you take an eyebrow-raising deep breath. This can be accomplished through diet and dance class. If you take only a few classes a week and chomp on chips, Twinkies, and fried chicken in between times, you will not tone your body; if you take class every day and eat smart, you will.

Since every person is different and I am not a nutritionist, I can't tell you what diet is best for you. By diet, I do not mean deprivation, I mean fuel. What combination of foods gives you energy but doesn't drop anchor in your fat cells? In my teen years the changes in my body suddenly turned my thighs from reeds to redwood trunks, but I didn't really notice the gradual weight gain until I compared myself to the other dancers in college. I found that cutting out carbohydrates worked wonders to lose weight, along with taking tons of dance classes. When cravings came, I walked through the grocery store, piling my cart with forbidden foods, and then would retrace my steps and put all the junk back on the shelves. Somehow, it satisfied me to pretend I owned the food for those few minutes. When I really wanted to pig out, I spent my precious savings on a huge hot fudge sundae, then took it home and poured it down the sink. I figured that swallowing those useless calories would be as wasteful as throwing the sundae—and my money—away. Weird, but it worked. Sculpting your body takes patience, experimenting, and truly being aware that nature will always hand you a new set of rules as your body grows. My suggestion is to listen to your body, give nature a chance before you freak out on fad diets, and please, don't resort to anorexic or bulimic tendencies.

GRACIELA DANIELE: Discipline at the Teatro Colón was incredible. It was like a convent or an Argentinean West Point where every detail of your life was regulated. What the teachers demanded physically from us was wonderful, and I don't regret a minute of it, but I was tired all the time. And hungry. Our weight was strictly watched. We were constantly reminded, "Get your belly in!" At twelve, we didn't even have bellies, for God's sake. I have a very protruding rib cage. They'd poke me with a cane to get my stomach in. It wasn't my stomach, it was my ribs! I thought I'd have to break my bones to be in the theatre. Then when I got boobies at puberty, I was very unhappy. I wanted to be flat chested like a man—the ideal of a ballet dancer. Yet, as much as we wanted to be thin, we were not as maniacal about weight as here in America. It was something to work on, but not an obsession.

CAITLIN CARTER: Being skinny was a big deal at some of my ballet schools growing up. They'd ask, "How tall are her parents? How much do they weigh?" to try to figure out what size you might end up being. They even asked for X-rays from my pediatrician. Going through puberty was so traumatic. I grew two inches and gained four pounds in one year, but at the weigh-ins they didn't look at the height change, only the weight gain. So I simply starved myself, like so many other dancers. At the North Carolina School of the Arts there was a cafeteria with amazing food, but only the musicians and other theatre departments would pig out. My eating for three years was one egg for breakfast and salad for lunch and dinner. I was borderline anorexic. When I would come home for Christmas vacation, my mother would tell me I had to expand my diet, so I'd read cookbooks and bake things but I'd never eat them. When I left ballet I grew two more inches, gained some weight, grew tits, and finally got my period back. At first I resented the extra weight and curves, but when I joined a jazz company it was a good look to have. I started to like it. And I finally ate a hamburger—something I hadn't had in eight years. Looking back, I wonder if the not eating is going to rear its ugly head when I'm fifty-five. Your teen years are so important. I keep thinking that it might come back to haunt me.

ROBERT MONTANO: At the racetrack I struggled to keep my weight down. I did everything I could from flipping my food, to taking drugs, to jogging ten to fifteen miles seven days a week. My daily intake was a cup of coffee and half a bran muffin in the morning, then salad with no dressing and half a glass of water to wash it down at 7 P.M. That was it! Every day—disciplined. After I ended my riding career, I ate normally and was surprised that I developed such energy and strength; something I wasn't used to.

Basic body structure is something you must deal with. You can't cut and paste your bones to make a shorter waist or longer legs, nor is it wise to resort to surgery to increase the look of your arch. For most dancers the curse of "bad feet" can become an obsession. Because high arches are architecturally beautiful to look at, we tend to judge dancers not on the strength of the foot, but on the size of the arch. One dancer I worked with didn't resort to surgery to alter the look of her feet, but to foam rubber. She was as strong as an ox, but her arches weren't very high. So for performances she bundled pieces of foam over the top of her feet. When she pointed, her feet looked okay, but when she stood flat, the shoe straps cut into the foam, making her feet look like bound pillows. Ridiculous. For Broadway, you need strength, not God-given perfection. Work in class on developing your body to the utmost, but don't fret over what you can't change.

BEBE NEUWIRTH: My feet were the bane of my existence. I spent a lot of time trying to improve—pointing my feet, or not, because it was so depressing. And there was a period of time when I went to sleep in passé to help my turnout. There were girls who were so beautiful, but I knew I would never be one of them. But I still worked very hard because I knew that being a professional dancer is not limited to classical ballet, Martha Graham, or Savion Glover's tap kids. There is an enormous variety of ways for a dancer to express themselves that are all equally valid. What you bring to these forms, how you express yourself, is the thing that will make you dance metaphorically and literally. I may not have the perfect body, but how come I got the jobs and the technician didn't? I think it's energy, focus, presence, and developing what you have been given as completely, fully, and respectfully as you can.

Proper dance training can alter your muscle structure to augment what is too skinny or slim what is too bulky. These parts of your body are definitely something you can change.

LUIS PEREZ: At my hometown studio our look didn't matter too much because nobody had that much of a beautiful body. We were just guys. But at the Joffrey we had guys with super long legs, hyperextended knees, and beautiful feet. I had good feet but not lean muscle. I was a runner, a football player, so my quads were huge and I had a thick upper body. I could really jump high but it was more like throwing a brick in the air. As time and training went on, those things lengthened out. My legs looked like they grew twelve inches. Of course, they didn't; the muscle changed. My waist went from a thirty-two to a twenty-nine and my upper body went from a thirty-six to a forty. I worked my feet until I could literally stand on pointe in bare feet and walk. Through work, my body reorganized itself.

DAVID WARREN-GIBSON: I was tall and felt sort of gangly, like I was always going to hit someone, but by taking class my thighs developed and my legs strengthened. What I had a rough time with were my hands. I had mitten hands—thumb all tensed out—so I worked for years on how to allow energy to flow through them. Now I love them. It's so important visually. When I see bad hands, even on good dancers, it really offends me.

Male dancers have a unique dilemma of body image in today's world of entertainment. With the boon of health clubs and six-pack abs in advertising, men may feel that a buff look is the answer to landing jobs. It is true that a muscular look is attractive and many dancers are being hired for their bulges. But the muscle mass prevents full mobility of movement, creating lines that are the antithesis to good technique, physical communication, and captivating visual image. As far as partnering goes, lifting a hundred-pound weight is not the same as lifting a woman. Partnering demands a sensitivity to proportions, weight distribution, and dynamics. A hundred-pound woman with long legs will feel completely different from a hundred-pound woman with shorter legs and wider hips. All the dumbbells in the world will not give you an inkling of real flesh and blood.

Unfortunately, there is a misconception among a growing number of dancers that a workout in the gym can replace dance classes. From a cosmetic viewpoint, it is understandable. Bodybuilding is hard to do, but a quick fix. Where it may take a year of dance classes to change a muscle group, a few days of pumping iron gives immediate results. Those pecs are round, firm, and lookin' fine when you do that constipated posing stuff. However, dance is an art form, not a muscle contest, and the only place to learn to be a complete dancer is in a dance class.

GRACIELA DANIELE: I notice more and more male dancers who have this great bulk—incredible bodies. But I don't look at that. I expect craft. I expect technique. And personality and individuality and imagination. These are qualities that come from inside, not from puffy muscles.

JIM BORSTELMANN: I work with the bodybuilders and they drop girls. They're bigger than me, they've got these muscles, and they're weak as shit. There is no dance training in a gym. Use a gym for toning, sure, but learn how to lift a girl correctly. People are going to the gym because it's fun and you look good. But then you get a guy onstage whose shoulders are up and he can't point his feet and he can't support a girl. A gym—that's not a teacher. My *name* is Jim and it ends there.

TOMMY TUNE: Growing up we didn't have gyms. The only gym in town was the Y and that had a bad reputation as a pickup spot. We didn't build ourselves like guys do today. It is a double-edged thing. For a certain type of show these built up bodies look great, like if the show takes place in Cuba and you have these muscular bodies with little clothing on. But for the guys who wear tails, like in *Follies,* big muscles don't let the clothes hang properly. They look like big blocks coming at you, whereas a thinner person looks just right. So it depends on type—the right type for a show.

DAVID WARREN-GIBSON: Big boobs, big pecs—it works, it sells. I like looking at it, the audience likes looking at it—who doesn't like to see a beautiful body that's worked out? If they have some talent going, too, that's great. Dance has certain lines, a certain technique, but it depends what you want to do. Because of the way the media is, if you want to sell your muscles and sell your sex, then, yeah, do it.

Women have a different dilemma with what is considered attractive, but we have so many more options to disguise what nature has given us than do men. Makeup highlights and shading, hair color, plucked brows, and clothing that can push up or pull in, all help to make your image more attractive. However, in this age of instant gratification, some young women are determined to rush their natural beauty by running to the ever cheaper plastic surgeons and dermatologists who can nip, suction, scrape, or reconstruct movie stars and department store clerks alike. I find it a shame to not let the duckling become the swan in its own good time. Unless you have an outstanding physical feature or scar that is truly inhibiting, have patience until you are at least in your mid-twenties before you consider altering your body artificially. If you are then determined to go from an A cup to a D, thinking it will enhance your marketability, go for it—though casting people may find more beauty in your dance ability and confidence than in your bust size.

JOANN M. HUNTER: I was a chunky monkey as a kid. As a female I already had that extra layer of fat, and then being half Japanese I had an extra, extra layer. That's a very general statement, but it's true. Asian women can tend to be a little bit doughier. Everything on me was round. But when I was twenty-four, I lost all of my baby fat and my muscle tone became tauter. My body changed completely. People thought I had reconstructive facial surgery because my face had naturally lengthened. Even my mother thought I had surgery! The only things that didn't change were my breasts. I've never had big boobs. But now I have my two water bras and I'm set.

MAMIE DUNCAN-GIBBS: My nose bothered other people, but it didn't bother me. It was mine, the nose I had my whole life. But it got in the way for a lot of jobs. My sister thought I was just paranoid until one day we were walking from 45th Street down to Macy's and people I did not know commented on my nose. A bum—this bum!—called out, "Got a big nose there!" Somebody else said, "Follow your nose!" In Macy's two little kids were running around and one of them stopped and said, "Hi, nose!" My sister couldn't believe it. I told her I went through this all the time. When I went to a call for *Sophisticated Ladies* the assistant who was running the audition told me after I sang, "The reason why you didn't get the job last time and the reason you're not getting it this time is because of your nose. I'm telling you this because you are so talented, but it's getting in your way. If you have it fixed, it will put you on the other side of glamorous." I paid her no mind, thinking, "Oh, she's only one person. Who's she? She's not Bob Fosse." I still wasn't getting jobs, but I didn't want to start changing things until I was absolutely sure that it wasn't my dancing that wasn't good enough. So I studied really hard and then auditioned for Bob Fosse for *Big Deal*. I was in great shape, doing triple pirouettes on a dime, but I heard him say, "She can dance, but look at her nose." I got cut. That's when I vowed to fix it. I told the doctor to only take out what was necessary because I still wanted to look like me. The next time I auditioned for Bob Fosse was for the national tour of *Sweet Charity* and I got the job. Later I auditioned again for *Sophisticated Ladies* and I got hired on the spot. I didn't take that job, but I was really happy to know that it wasn't my talent that had stopped me in the past.

Apart from the outer image, you should take care of your body beneath the skin. There is no doubt that dance hurts as you stretch and strengthen your muscles. But there is a huge difference between a "good" hurt and a "bad" hurt. While a broken bone is pretty self-evident, the "bad" hurt of a strain, sprain, or tear of the muscles, ligaments, and cartilage can be tempting to ignore. Do not let blind determination stop you from going to a doctor, chiropractor, kinesiologist, or physical therapist to check out an unusually insistent pain. Treat yourself to hot baths and massage. You want your body—your instrument—to last a long time, and often a little TLC can make the difference between a temporary injury or a debilitating one.

Because our language is movement, dancers often have to muster untapped energy reserves to get through a class, rehearsal, or show. Some dancers unwisely turn to drugs to get them through, especially amphetamines and cocaine, which stimulate the nervous system and ward off hunger at the same time. While I know many performers who traveled the drug route feeling wired and invincible, I know of no one who didn't experience the inevitable crash of depression, paranoia, and burnout that accompany sustained use. Personally I sampled both uppers and cocaine and knew immediately to stay away from them because the false energetic allure could so easily become an unhealthy trap, not to mention the financial drain. There is a far higher sense of accomplishment and reward if you face difficult times with only true self-determination as your comrade. Sure, you may feel dog tired at some point, but by relying only on yourself, you build stamina, knowledge, and pride.

No matter the walls you may encounter that block your dream of dancing on Broadway, determination will help you over, under, around, or smash through the negativity. This is your dream, your life, and no one has the right to stop you, well intentioned or not. Never lose heart. Everyone who has danced to the beat, whether onstage, in the movies, or on MTV, has been where you are today. Their very presence and success in the world is a testament to the important, artistic, and inspirational profession you wish to enter. Your next step is to be sure you have the right teachers to guide you closer to your dream.

CHAPTER THREE

The Never-ending Quest: Teachers and Technique

Teachers are so important. The best teachers don't just teach 1, 2, 3, 4 but guide you—how to audition, the love they have for the profession, humility, respect. It is so appreciated. It enriches you.

— Julio Monge

Dance Teachers and Studios

Dance teachers will be with you for your whole professional life. You will progress from your hometown studios to college or directly to New York, constantly perfecting your craft. A good dance teacher can come in a variety of flavors. There are the teachers for different styles—jazz, ballet, tap, modern, character, partnering, and ballroom to name a few. There are teachers who quietly coax, teachers who hit you with canes and poke you with hat pins, teachers who take you under their wings, and teachers whose modus operandi is to not smile at a new student for the first three months. Some teachers work in dusty garrets and some conduct class in brilliant studios. The important thing to remember is that the student/teacher relationship is not a personality contest. You must look for a teacher who spurs you to constantly improve, no matter the method. A really good teacher will recognize your desire and help you in any way they can.

MAMIE DUNCAN-GIBBS: Frank Hatchett taught at the Dunbar Community Center, where I took gymnastics. He saw how I hung around the studio all the time so one day he offered me free classes. I was like, "I can't dance." And he said, "Well, you walk like a duck. You can dance." He gave me free classes for a year without my mother knowing. When I moved to New York I didn't have any money. I called Frank at JoJo's Dance Factory and he gave me free classes for two years. Two years! He has helped so many people. He sure saved me.

CHITA RIVERA: When I went for my audition for the School of American Ballet at fourteen years old, I stepped off the elevator holding hands with my teacher, Miss Jones, and we heard this cry, "Oh, God!" and this young girl comes crying, running from a studio. I stopped dead in my tracks as I heard in the background, "Yuck! Uck!" I looked at Miss Jones and she said, "Go straight ahead. Just deal with yourself. Don't let anything frighten you or stop you. Just go!" We went right into the locker room and found the girl crying in the corner. She had been in class with Mr. Obukhov. He was a killer. In the following years when I had Mr. Obukhov he scared me, but I didn't cry. I was more of a fighter, I think. One time he knocked me off my attitude relevé—just pushed me and said, "Yuck!" I hit the piano. Well, I thought that was the funniest thing that somebody actually pushed me at all! So I bounced off the piano, came right back, and hit the attitude again. All the kids gasped. Today they would've applauded, but back then you wouldn't dare. You wouldn't make a sound in those days. I like it that way.

JOANN M. HUNTER: My teacher stressed ballet. Her point was that it is your base, like learning the alphabet. If you can do ballet, you can do anything. She was strict—really tough. Oh, she would take that stick and . . . But I'd rather have a teacher correct me than ignore me. What am I paying for if a teacher is not going to look at me? Some people today don't want the correction. They want to get to the end of a jazz class where you do the little dance combination. But if you aren't told what you are doing wrong, how do you learn?

Often good teachers can say something aside from technique that sticks with you forever. Among the many wonderful teachers I have had, starting with Jane DeFalco in Worcester, Massachusetts, and continuing with

Sandra Philpott at the Hazel Boone Studios outside Boston, two have particularly altered my life with comments that they probably don't even remember saying. One was a teacher at The Boston Conservatory whom I didn't particularly like. Upon graduation I was tempted to take the scholarship and apprentice programs I was offered at Joffrey and ABT and she said to me, "You have brilliant technique, but no soul. Go to Europe and learn how to breathe." I hated her! Yet I grudgingly, perhaps subconsciously, followed her advice, indeed learned to live movement through the exceptional French, Italian, and Russian ballet masters I had with Les Ballets de Marseille de Roland Petit, and now bless her for her insight. The other teacher was Wilson Morrelli in New York City. I loved his ballet class, but it was one of those days when I was feeling ill, useless, untalented, and frustrated—every pirouette and piqué felt just plain off. He showed no sympathy as I struggled my way through class, blurry-eyed with tears, and seemed to goad me with more corrections than usual. At the end of class he pulled me aside and said, "First, you didn't give up. Second, if you can look that good when you are feeling so lousy, you've reached a level of true technique. What you think is your worst is better than other people's best. Believe it and rely on it at the worst of times." Time after time since then his words have given me courage and focus.

DAVID WARREN-GIBSON: I took ballet classes at SMU while I was still in high school. There was a Russian teacher there who offered me a scholarship if I forgot about going to high school, painting, playing the piano, everything. He was great, but he was from the very Old World thinking that if you danced, you just danced. Another Russian teacher said, "We have an expression in Russia: A man who chases too many rabbits, catches none." And I thought, "Oh yeah? It may take a little longer but I'll catch 'em all."

ROBERT MONTANO: My mentor, Norman Walker, was the artistic director of Adelphi's dance department. In the beginning he and I didn't see eye-to-eye since I came from the racetrack world where I saw everything mainly in black and white, while Norman came from an artistic, classical standpoint where it's mostly gray. He would dismantle me with a witty, soft elegance, saying stuff like, "My dear, I always see you practicing the things you do well. Why don't you practice the things that you don't?" or "I see you relaxing and laughing it up in the wings. You're not that good yet. Concentrate!" He even gave me an ultimatum: "Either you gallop horses or you dance. Choose. Your legs are bowed, you have no turnout, plus you come into the studio with horse manure on your boots. Enough!" He was harsh, but he prepared me for this highly competitive profession where only the tough survive. He taught me how to dance, listen, and to see things a bit more in gray.

A teacher who seems right for you today may not be the one for you a year from now. Likewise, a teacher you can't stand may tomorrow be your hero. Whoever helps you the most to master as much technique as possible before coming to New York is the right teacher for you. Don't be afraid to compare and expand. Take class at different studios, colleges, summer dance camps, or dance conventions and compare yourself to people from outside your home studio. You will gain insight from new teachers, see your future competition, and be able to determine if you are up to snuff in a larger pool before diving into the competitive ocean of Broadway.

TOMMY TUNE: What happened was that around high school age I needed to spread my wings. I was getting itchy about just learning the same things from my teachers. So I would go to see other recitals and ask the dancers I liked where they took class. I think I was breaking my true dancing teacher's heart by taking class elsewhere. But I always returned to my teachers after I had my fling with the others—like an affair. They were a part of my life. My original teacher, Emmamae Horn, was a woman of amazing imagination with ideas. The cowgirls, or Dogies as we called them, in *The Will Rogers Follies*? Their costumes are straight from Miss Horn, from a number she did called the "Cow Cow Boogie." I asked her permission to put them in the show and she said, "I forgot about that. Yeah, go ahead." I was vilified for those costumes. "Women as meat, Mr. Tune?" My goodness! It was simply a steal from this wonderful little dancing teacher in Texas.

LUIS PEREZ: I knew Edith Royal's was a good school because she already had three male principals in the Joffrey, another guy who was a principal in Las Vegas, and Ronn Forella, who was a major jazz dancer and teacher in New York. Her track record was impeccable and she was president of Dance Masters of America. A lot of the kids would ask her advice and she would tell parents, "If your son wants to dance, this is a good college where he can still get an education" or "She has the talent to take that scholarship with the company." She never crushed anybody's dreams but she was honest.

Once you make the move to New York City, you will find scores of studios and hundreds of classes taught by hundreds of teachers that run on an ongoing basis. You pay per class or buy a dance card at a discount for an average of ten classes. You may hook up with a teacher who takes a personal interest in your progress or you may take class with a teacher who appreciates your commitment and progress but may never know your name. It is your choice to take whatever level class is offered from beginner to advanced, unless it is a closed professional class. You will find superb dancers in a beginner's class because they want to get back to basics or are recovering from an injury, and you will find wanna-bes flailing their way through the advanced class. Certain extraordinary teachers offer only a few classes, so if you want to study with them, you may find yourself out of your league. My suggestion is to try whatever classes seem to fit you from your perception, and then ask the teachers if they think this is where you belong. Good teachers will either tell you to come back because they think they can help you or will suggest another class. A money-grubber will say, "Come back anytime, darling," keep collecting your money, and never give you the time of day. On the whole, if you show honest commitment to trying your best, you will get the support you need.

If you are already in New York City and can't find a place to take class, you'd better check your airline ticket to see if you landed in the right city. It is as simple as looking in the Yellow Pages or reading the ads in *Dance Magazine*. More adventurous ways are to look up when you hear music and see if there are dancers in the windows or to follow anyone carrying a dancebag. Exactly which studio to go to is a matter of taking single classes here and there and seeing where you feel the best. Don't worry about looking like an idiot. Until you become known in the Broadway circle, you are truly anonymous.

Dance Technique and Styles

The initial style a dancer chooses is one that attracts the spirit and speaks to the soul. The eagerness to master the moves is the propulsion to lay down the first ten bucks for a class. As a Broadway dancer, however, you need to expand your knowledge, no matter how fascinated you are with one particular style. Broadway choreographers come from all dance worlds, and each show, and the numbers within each show, will run the stylistic gamut. The more varied you are, the more marketable you will become.

While all styles give you strength, flexibility, dynamics, and balance, each style (and each style within each style) hones in on certain aspects. In a very broad sense: Tap teaches you extraordinary percussion, both with your feet and in understanding rhythm in music. Jazz addresses isolations, parallel positions, stylized pedestrian movement, musical theatre, and funk. Modern teaches you physical design and dynamics in space. Ballroom encompasses all forms of social dancing, and when advanced, superior partnering. Gymnastics deals with balance, flexibility, and really cool flips and tricks. And ballet . . .

Ballet is the mother of all. Although one can argue that the cavemen hopped and grunted around a campfire long before the French started calling a hop a "sauté," the rules of ballet are what all the other styles broke. We are talking about dance as a profession—a profession like any other with rules and concepts of what constitutes excellence. The best dancers know the rules of ballet and are masters at breaking them. I do not suggest that ballet dancers are superior to Broadway dancers. Believe me, I've performed in both worlds and have heard snooty remarks from both sides. It is true that not many Broadway dancers would make the best Giselle. But few ballerinas can perform "Music and the Mirror" from *A Chorus Line* with a semblance of credibility. Sing, act, and do all those layouts? Not on your life.

GRACIELA DANIELE: When I lived in Paris, we ballerinas would pooh-pooh some of the dancers in the Folies Bergère but certainly that stopped when I saw *West Side Story.* I had never seen a musical before and all I could think was, "I've got to go to New York to learn how to do that."

BEBE NEUWIRTH: I have found that some people can be really arrogant about their own branch of dance. There are ballet dancers who are arrogant about ballet and modern dancers who are arrogant about modern. One modern dancer actually said to me that theatre dance was not real dancing! We should learn to recognize and respect the value of every style. There are ballet dancers who make fantastic modern or jazz dancers and some jazz dancers who are wonderful in ballet. I saw this kid in ballet class the other day and thought, "Who is this boy? He's beautiful!" Well, he has his own Hip-Hop company.

Personal preference aside, you need to take ballet, like it or not. Not exclusively—dance should never be penance—but the sooner, the better.

MAMIE DUNCAN-GIBBS: I thought ballet sucked because I was a jazz baby. At auditions I kept getting cut after the ballet combination and they didn't get to see my jazz. So I was really good about studying ballet no matter how much I hated it. You've got to deal with the ballet because you need it. It's like learning classical music on the piano. You don't just sit down and start playing the blues. You learn the basics that you can apply to the blues. When a dancer applies ballet to jazz, it's fabulous.

JULIO MONGE: In Puerto Rico we were more in awe of dance than technique. In our culture we dance for any excuse. At a party you don't get the eggnog and sit in a corner. You dance. At the studio I loved jazz. It's loose with hot music and if you are not so good, you don't get intimidated. But ballet is not so pleasant. I am thankful for it, but at the time? Please. The développé? How hurtful is that for a boy? And the vocabulary is so hard when you are starting. "Eh? Tendu-who? Déga-what? You want me to hold what? In the air? My leg to the front, the side, the back, and then bring it back again? Are you crazy?" I knew ballet was the foundation so I struggled with it. Now I do it better. It's a way of shaping my dance. It is not the end, just the means. So what if I don't have perfect turnout. The exercise itself is helping my muscles to get longer, not wider. I just wish I was good enough to show off a little.

DAVID WARREN-GIBSON: I had to practice tap constantly because I felt I was behind everyone else. Ballet was different. I didn't know what the hell I was doing but the piano and the music—it just went into my bones. It just amazed me what the dancers could do with their bodies and the passion of it and the dedication and the sweat. I loved it. Of course, there's that serious part of standing at the barre. "Whoa! I can't play around. I really have to do this now." I came to love doing barre. It was my support—something to cling on to. Once I got off to come center, I felt like Bambi on the ice. Whoa!

<u>Caitlin Carter:</u> Jazz doesn't do it all. Everyone in a ballet class knows exactly why they're there, what they're supposed to be doing. Jazz is looser. Which is not a bad thing. You have much more fun. But there are elements of ballet that I wish you could find in musical theatre—just honoring the choreography as one would in a ballet.

<u>Michael Kubala:</u> I studied jazz twice a week, a half hour each time. Then I added tap but I didn't like the fundamentals of it—the fa-lap, fa-lap, fa-lap, fa-lap, ba-dum, ba-dum . . . I just wanted to go br-r-r-r-r-r-r like a machine gun. I loved jazz—the jump splits and head rolls and isolations and being totally wild. Anything I thought was difficult or awe-inspiring I enjoyed doing. But in ballet class, I felt clumsy. In my first class I was scared and sweating and remember being very pulled up, but not knowing what I was doing. I knew some basic terms from jazz class but the arms, all those positions, were hard for me. I just kept my arms in second or above my head. Then the changements and the beats. Whooo! That was like being stuck in a blender. And the stretching was painful. I'd say to my teacher, "This hurts. Let's just bop."

When most dancers think about dance on Broadway, they think jazz. This is entirely true if you consider that jazz encompasses every style of dance throughout the decades infused with the rudiments of ballet. All jazz classes vary in the explanation and molding of a solid technique and unfortunately are often "fierce" without furthering an expansive technique. Although some dancers who have an innate sense of their bodies can learn jazz moves through imitation, the best jazz teachers understand the technique behind each shoulder roll, hip thrust, and flick kick, and truly teach how to execute them. After all, the human body is a compilation of movable parts, and in each style those parts simply move in a different order and extent. The fact is, you need jazz; you need flair; you need to be able to pop into a Lindy or Shim-Sham as easily as a pencil turn to a jazz split. My suggestion is to vary your jazz classes among those that address a solid technical style, those that offer historical or theatrical repertory styles, and those that are more contemporary. Also, with each show you do, you will accumulate the feel for a multitude of styles, both historically and choreographically.

<u>Chita Rivera:</u> Peter Gennaro was the first person who taught me a contraction, my first thing with jazz. He gave me my fast feet. Then Augie

and Margo wanted to study ballet and I wanted to learn Afro-Cuban so I introduced them to SAB and they took me over to the Dunham school. I saw Geoffrey Holder for the first time and he had this steel band. I had never seen one before. My world opened up so wide. In one jazz class at Carnegie Hall, Marlon Brando played conga drums. It was those days when we all were studying, broadening our horizons.

Modern is not typically performed on Broadway, but you never know. More and more modern choreographers choreograph Broadway shows and your knowledge of the language just might get you the job. Modern is fantastic in developing an awareness of your body in space and how to travel through space. It helps you to use your center both on and off balance, to extend your lines, to heighten your elevation, and to think in more three-dimensional terms. There are so many styles of modern, investigate wisely which attracts you. As with ballet, you may like it or not, but even a few classes will broaden your technique.

JIM BORSTELMANN: At first I didn't like modern. I thought it smelled. Every girl had hairy armpits. And the bare feet and the body types and the scary punk hairdos. Boy, was I wrong. I ended up dancing in two modern dance companies. One was in the style of Limón. I loved it. But modern had that kooky music. One time I had to come out in a tutu with combat boots.

GRACIELA DANIELE: When I came here, I studied jazz with Matt Mattox. I tried a couple of modern classes at Martha Graham, but Matt said that for me, I'd be better at Merce Cunningham. He was right.

BEBE NEUWIRTH: The sexuality of different kinds of dance is very important to me. Ballet is sexy because it is romantic, a fairy-tale kind of sexuality. Jazz is more erotic sex. It's a little bit lower—you're doing it. I took some modern classes but it didn't resonate within any realm of my sexuality, not the romantic or the erotic or the elegant. That's not to say it won't make sense to someone else because we are all so different. My sense is that modern is built from a basic human movement—which couldn't be more sexual—but too often there's an intellectual "something" imposed on that basic human instinct.

Tap was at one time a main staple of Broadway fare. Both Broadway and the films of the '20s, '30s, and '40s had tapping stars, surrounded by throngs of clickety clacking chorus people. Nowadays, tap is not as prevalent, but it certainly is represented in revivals and specialized shows like *Bring in 'Da Noise, Bring in 'Da Funk* and *Tap Dogs*. Tommy Tune and Susan Stroman often choreograph tap into their shows, and in many shows tap vocabulary is used without actually having tap shoes on. The feeling of tap is so totally different from other forms of dance, it is worthwhile to have a handle on the basics. Although I was in only one show where I wore tap shoes, countless times I was thankful for having a solid feel for tap technique. While other dancers struggled to execute the steps without looking earthbound, for me it was a breeze.

<u>CAITLIN CARTER</u>: I didn't tap well when I first came to New York but within the first two weeks I got *Ain't Broadway Grand*. I was shocked. From the waist up I looked like I knew what I was doing, but I faked it. Since then I've taken some tap classes, but my tapping skills have improved for the most part from doing shows.

<u>EUGENE FLEMING</u>: When I got *Sophisticated Ladies* I got to put on my tap shoes. I hadn't worn tap shoes since I was a kid and I didn't even remember that I could tap. I went and studied a little bit with Henry LeTang to get the style back, and I guess I had enough of the basic vocabulary to just go in and do the show. After *Sophisticated Ladies* I went to Rome to do a television show with Harold Nicholas, and then came back to take over the lead in *Tap Dance Kid*. Tap, together with my solid ballet training and the fact that I could sing, has made me a truly versatile performer.

Ballroom dance is worth its weight in gold to round out your technique. A major plus is that you get to dance with someone else. Let's take a look at history. Up until the 1960s people danced together socially. Whether it was a formal minuet in European courts, a rigorous Virginia reel in the countryside, a twirling waltz during the Civil War, a smooth Foxtrot on the *Titanic*, a wild Charleston in a speakeasy, a romping Jitterbug at the Savoy, or a hip-flinging Boogie to "Rock and Roll Is Here to Stay," partners danced and delighted together as one unit. They sensed each other's rhythm, weight, and balance, improvising securely on the spur of the moment. With the introduction of the dance crazes of the disco era, all of a sudden everyone was Frugging and Jerking into a frenzy, but no one was touching anymore except to drape in a boring sway during slow songs. Real partnering was only for nerds. Since then, the Hustle, *Dirty Dancing*, John Travolta, the reemergence of Tango, Western dancing, and all of the fabulous Hispanic dances have caused a resurrection in the art of social dance partnering.

For the professional dancer, partnering classes are few and far between except in college dance programs and concert dance companies, yet on Broadway today partnering is making a comeback with such shows as *Swing*, *Contact*, and in the many revivals. Wherever you can find a partnering class, grab it for all it's worth. If none are available, all around the country there are ballroom dance studios where you can take class and tons of clubs where you can practice moves with a partner. In New York City there are many ballroom studios, one in particular being Pierre DuLaine's Dance Club. Besides being a four-time winner of the World Exhibition Championship and on the faculties of the School of American Ballet and Juilliard, Pierre and his partner, Yvonne Marceau, wowed audiences in the musical *Grand Hotel*. As such, they truly understand the needs of theatre dancers. Even a few classes will broaden your technique. As good as you may be dancing alone, you will be much more valuable if you understand ballroom vocabulary and can feel unified with the heartbeat of another person.

JULIO MONGE: When I grew up in Puerto Rico, we danced Salsa all the time. I'm thankful for it. There is the Mambo section of *West Side Story* in *Jerome Robbins' Broadway* and I thought, "Piece of cake." I think that's what got me the job, really. Even though later in the show I had to do "Tradition." Oy vey, a Puerto Rican Jew.

CHITA RIVERA: The Palladium was extraordinary. The Harry Belafontes and Lena Hornes—all of these stars—were sitting around, Augie and Margo danced, and the Latin men came dressed, looking fabulous. One night I went with a friend and there was a dance contest on. This big, tall Watusi had asked me to dance and all of a sudden we got a tap on the shoulder that we were in the contest. There I was, this naive Catholic chorus girl, dancing with this guy who was making me do these brilliant partnering moves. I mean, you get involved! With the music going and going, I decided to take off and started doing piqué turns around this poor guy. I must have looked like an idiot. But we won! I guess they figured anybody who's got that kind of nerve . . .

Character classes are helpful to, in a good sense, make you un-American. We do not have a singular national dance that comes from our roots since we are such a melting pot of nationalities, but in many shows we must perform as citizens of another country. Look at *Evita*, *Fiddler on the Roof*, and *Zorba!*, just to name a few. Many studios offer character classes, but class isn't necessarily the only place to observe dance styles. Folk dance troupes perform at colleges, festivals, and parades. If you want to have a great time, go to Greek, Israeli, Spanish, Irish, any ethnic restaurant or club where they have music. Many times they have performers, or normal people just get up and start dancing the "real" thing. Once you've got the hang of what they're doing and if you've got the guts, join in. It's not only a blast, but you will also gain an appreciation of the finesse, meaning, and vitality of these dances.

MICHAEL KUBALA: I took character class at a dance camp, clicking the heels and all that. It seemed hokey in the beginning, but I got into it. If I had known all those styles I learned were going to be such an integral part of what I do now, I would have had a much firmer appreciation, understanding, and enjoyment of it. Diversification is the key.

You may already be involved with gymnastics and sports. While these are not necessary to become a Broadway dancer, they can be helpful.

LUIS PEREZ: By the time I was really into ballet, I didn't play football anymore. I didn't want to risk a broken knee or anything like that. So I became a cheerleader. We had a really cool coach who taught us a lot of lifts and gymnastic moves. I still use them.

MAMIE DUNCAN-GIBBS: I've gotten jobs because I could do the walkover or the flip. It didn't always matter, but it helped.

JIM BORSTELMANN: Sports—played everything. Basketball helped me get that extra little lift in a jump and dribbling got me a job in a movie. When I did *Damn Yankees*, catching a baseball and doing that thing with the mitt was easy for me, but some guys couldn't do it. I think sports help your coordination, your mind, and your discipline.

JULIO MONGE: I was very athletic and played some sports, but sports are a different vibe. There's no applause at the end; it's all about being rough, the toughest, especially in Puerto Rico where sports like boxing, baseball, and basketball are so important. I played all of them, but I liked performing better because there is a reward from the audience.

JOANN M. HUNTER: I was stiff so gymnastics absolutely helped me, especially taking from Chuck Kelly. Oh my God, he would take your legs and stretch them for minutes at a time until you thought they would break right off. But gymnastics limbered up my back and gave me upper-body strength, which really helps in partnering and lifts. A lot of women who have never partnered think, "Just pick me up." They have no idea that it's about timing and strength. You have to work as hard as a man in a lift.

Hip-Hop is finding its way into shows with a contemporary theme, not to mention the deluge in music videos, television, and film. Some dancers who are proficient also earn terrific money teaching Hip-Hop classes in their free time. The only caution is not to make Hip-Hop your strongest selling point, but rather a wonderful sideline to your technical base.

JULIO MONGE: At first I looked at Hip-Hop with suspicion. Was it really working at a technique? I felt breaking on the floor was rather clownish. Being exposed to New York and seeing where it was really coming from and seeing some really good ones here, I thought, "It is dance. These are real artists and it's exhilarating. It's as good as any dance technique when it's done well."

By this point you may be tearing your hair out thinking, "I can't take all of these classes! The time, the money . . ." Of course, you don't have to run yourself ragged. Your diversification does not have to be complete before you hop a plane to New York, and your training will span a lifetime. What I intend to stress is that a truly valuable Broadway dancer locks down ballet and jazz and shuns no other style. Being a jack of all trades and a master of one will buy you the security that no matter what is thrown at you in an audition or rehearsal, you will handle it with confidence. Take your time. Master what you can while you keep your eyes and mind open to opportunities to sample the styles that are not your primary courses of study. Each little bite will add up to a full meal of expertise that will make you technically solid, marketable, and valuable to choreographers, no matter how different they may be.

However, while you can spread your dance diversification over a long period of time, know that dance is not all that is needed to perform on Broadway. In the next chapter I lay out for you the other aspects of training that you will be wise to squeeze in to your day.

CHAPTER FOUR

Talent Is a Triple Threat

Going back to Mr. Joffrey, of course a good dancer needs talent. The dictionary defines *talent* as "a special natural ability or aptitude." Talent does not have to go as far as being extraordinarily gifted, as if Terpsichore kissed your feet the moment they slid out of the womb. Many a working dancer is technically proficient without being a crackerjack. The key words are *ability* and *aptitude*.

Some people think that natural ability means being able to do something well on the first try. A two-year-old throws a baseball two feet away and proud Papa says, "Hey! Look at that kid. He's a natural!" It's a bunch of bull. Sure, the toddler may have the ability to be the next Babe Ruth, but in most cases ability is developed through time and practice. Everyone feels the click—the understanding, the coordination—at different times. It's the click that counts.

There *is* such a thing as a natural dancer; they have a gift of movement in any style. Try as you might, you can't put your finger on exactly what they do that makes them such a joy to watch. From somewhere inside they know that tilting their head one-quarter-inch more will complete the picture and speak a thousand words. This ability cannot be taught. Imitated, yes. Taught, no. But don't fret. You may envy this ability, but you can work without it. This is where aptitude comes in to play. Formal dance demands that you force your body into unnatural positions with grace to a rhythm. This takes years of muscle training and keen observation of yourself and other dancers. If you have the aptitude to recognize, learn, and steadily progress, you will be a good dancer.

Aptitude is also a readiness to learn not only dance technique, but also all the aspects of theatre that make you a complete Broadway performer.

Dance aside, let's look at the other talents you should develop to become a triple threat on Broadway: singing, acting, and lumping all three together, performance quality, both on and off the stage. I'm not talking about singing like Barbara Streisand and acting like Laurence Olivier, but rather having a good grasp of these aspects of musical theatre. In an audition you will definitely be asked to sing and you may have to cold read. If you have never sung you are bound to choke up, and if you have never spoken out loud, something as simple as saying, "Mail's here!" could feel like a soliloquy. Your goal is to land a show and then build a career on Broadway. Cultivating your triple-threat talents will let you enjoy your career to its fullest capacity.

Singing

What a heartbreak it is when a fantastic dancer auditions but can't sing a note. Yet this happens quite often, especially when the dancer is making a switch to Broadway from concert dance. In the past, musicals had two separate choruses—the dancing chorus and the singing chorus—but finances today dictate the need for smaller casts. To further aid costs, understudies for roles are assigned to capable chorus members rather than have many off-stage covers. Within the show, many solo lines that would formerly be given to a singing chorus member are sung by dancers. Some shows don't demand singing, but it is very rare. The reality is, you must know how to sing. If you haven't yet developed this ability by studying, working in local theatres, or singing in school or church groups, get thee to a vocal teacher pronto! Not only will you develop your voice, but you will also become familiar with keys, tempos, time signatures, scales, and harmony.

CHITA RIVERA: When I first came to Broadway singing never entered my life. Shows always had the *Oklahoma!* thing—the singers on their knees at the footlights and the dancers in a sit-lift behind them. Then there was an audition for *Shoe String Revue* and someone said to me, "I'm not going to that audition because they want you to sing and dancers don't sing." I said, "What do you mean we don't sing? We talk. We can do something." So I went even though I had nothing prepared to sing. They said, "Sing anything." So I sang a commercial for Rinso White. Talk about having guts! I think you are in some kind of altered state when you go into a singing audition. Then that other thing takes over that says, "I'm here. I'm in this moment. Do this! Don't run." I don't think dancers run. They go for it.

GRACIELA DANIELE: I expect that a dancer is at least going to carry a tune. The quality, the amount of training, is not a priority as long as they have spark, energy, and sing on pitch. However, in some auditions I make a bargain with the musical director. If I see a dancer that is so extraordinary I can't live without the dancer in a show, I say to the musical director, "Okay, you can have the dodo who sings if I can have the good dancer who doesn't sing that well." Of course, the most important thing in this type of compromise is what kind of show it is, whether it is a dancing show or it requires a lot of singing.

Don't ever think you can't sing. The muscles of your throat and diaphragm are just like any other in your body. At first you may sound weak and off-key, but with training in breathing, placement, and tonality you will be amazed at how well you can handle a song. Granted, there are some people who are tone deaf, but give yourself the benefit of training before classifying yourself in this category.

BEBE NEUWIRTH: I believe that the only hurdle that dancers have in learning how to talk or sing onstage is getting used to the sound of our own voice. It's such an unnatural phenomenon, it really throws us and makes us very, very self-conscious. All the time that you spend in dance class, you spend with your mouth shut. There's no talking in class and then when you're performing in concert dance, nobody talks. You don't talk back to the teacher. They tell you what to do and you listen and do it. Then you get onstage in an audition or a show and you're asked to sing or speak. You are in this world that up until that point has been mute. So you do it and there's the sound of your own voice and it doesn't feel right. It's noise to our ears; it's as basic as that. Once we get used to the fact that it's okay to talk, we'll be fine.

The more you familiarize yourself with the music in past and current Broadway shows, the further you will be ahead of the game. Start your own library of CDs, or if you can't afford that, borrow the scores from the library, your dance teachers, or friends. Learn the lyrics to many songs and sing along to the recordings. If you have never sung before, this gives you a chance to have some privacy while you control your nerves. Eventually you will wean your way off the CDs; the loneliness of a piano and you in an audition is the future reality.

Once you have chosen a few songs, buy or borrow the sheet music and work with a vocal coach to find a good key. Warning: the key that the sheet music is written in is usually not the same key as on the recordings, so finding and notating your key is imperative. Once you have ironed out the technical problems with your teacher, have him tape a clean (nonvocal) copy so you can practice at home. You don't want to be locked into singing along to your own voice, as good or bad as it might be.

Your search for a vocal coach or voice teacher is quite simple. Many advertise in *Back Stage* if you are in the New York, Chicago, or Los Angeles area, and around the country some advertise in the Yellow Pages under "Music Instruction—Vocal." Ask other musical performers and directors for recommendations or talk to class and audition pianists. Just as you shop around for dance teachers, you will soon find a voice teacher that you like, and if you feel uncomfortable, keep looking. I went to my first "legitimate" voice teacher while performing in *A Chorus Line*. She was a boozy-breathed old opera dame who made me blow feathers around the room while intoning Gregorian chants for the first three lessons. Ask me if I took a fourth.

TOMMY TUNE: I didn't have very good luck with singing teachers. There are so many charlatans out there. Dancing, somehow, if you have an eye for it, you kind of know if a teacher is good or not because you can look at it and assess it. Singing? It's all this little stuff down in your throat. And everybody has a different idea of what singing is. Is it "a string of spaghetti coming out of your mouth"? And then you have to "Squeeze your buttocks together" or "Make a white square right in front of your lips" and not say, "White," but "Hoo-wh-ite." I mean, all these theories about what it is! Finally I just sang my heart out.

JIM BORSTELMANN: I knew I had to sing. So I did the same thing I did with watching dance—I listened to all sorts of music growing up and imitated the styles. I had a few voice lessons in Buffalo and learned about the vocal bands and stuff, and took dance-singers at STEPS in New York about three times where everyone sits in a group and sings. But mostly I learned to sing when I started getting shows.

ROBERT MONTANO: While performing in *Cats* my voice developed, but I didn't really begin to feel confident until I worked with Chita Rivera in her act, *Chita Plus Two*. She gave me latitude, strength, and the confidence to go out there and sing on my own.

Hopefully you will accrue a series of vocal exercises from your teacher to strengthen your voice and help you with your breathing. From a dancer's viewpoint, the breathing is a thorny affair. We dance with our ribs pulled down and our stomachs in. Years of training make this position second nature. To sing, the diaphragm must expand so air can fill the entire chest cavity. How can you look good dancing while you sing if your chest feels like a beer barrel and your belly a balloon? Breaking the habit of dance posture is difficult, but with time and practice you will find a happy medium.

Singing Audition Material

Be open to many types of songs with your voice teacher, but remember to work on audition material. The whole reason to prepare songs is to get you through an audition and into a show. Once you are in a show, the musical director will guide you through the new songs, sections, and harmonies you will perform in group numbers. But in an audition it's solo time. Sometimes sixteen bars are all the casting people need to judge you, but other times they want an entire song. These are precious moments that will determine whether you get the job. The more prepared, comfortable, and confident you are, the less it will feel like you are being sized up by the Spanish Inquisition.

The basics you will need are an up-tempo (a lively song from a Broadway show or movie musical, usually belted or blended) and a ballad to show your ability to sustain notes. The sound of Broadway is much more varied nowadays, from Rodgers and Hammerstein to *Rent*, so it is a tough decision to narrow yourself down to the one song that will best show your abilities. However, keep in mind what a musical director is really looking for in a dancer—good pitch, a solid range within the type of voice, and the ability to blend. The richness of the future vocal arrangements depends on these qualities. Remember that you are initially auditioning to be in the chorus of a show, so wailing a rock solo won't tell the musical director what he needs to know.

<u>EUGENE FLEMING</u>: I had only two songs in my repertoire and for a large while they were the only ones I used. My friends would joke with me. They'd see me coming and start singing my song, "Don't Get Around Much Anymore." That was my up-tempo and my ballad. I have a friend who knows a hundred songs but she hasn't perfected any of them. She can sing, but she doesn't have control over the songs. For me, I know I can't give my best if I'm not comfortable and in control.

<u>JOANN M. HUNTER</u>: My voice teacher helps me pick my songs. I trust her so much, I feel she will pick what's right for me. Sometimes I'll tell her that I want to do a song with a certain feel and she'll look through her library of music to give me three or four choices. Then we figure out which one I can handle. By now I probably have thirty songs in my repertoire—standard Broadway, contemporary Broadway, Gershwin, Cole Porter, Rodgers and Hammerstein. I have only two rock songs because I feel like a white girl when I have to sing rock. For an audition there are only a few that I sing most, but if they ask for something else, I'm ready.

Certain shows do request a specific style of song. Learning these styles at the last minute is dangerous because they won't be mastered. While you work on your traditional Broadway song, consider filtering in these other valuable components to your repertoire: a pop sound in the vein of Frank Wildhorn or Michael John LaChiusa shows, a '50s or '60s rock song, and a country-western. These specific styles have different demands on vocal placement and performance quality. Otherwise, rest assured that your Broadway tune will suffice. Choosing that particular song boils down to five factors:

1. The song must be securely within your vocal range. If a high note is hit or miss, nervous adrenaline may help you out when you are under the gun, but it's risky. That one missed note may erase all the landed ones. Your voice teacher can help you stretch your range over time and will tell you when to breathe for maximum effect and efficiency.

2. Figure out how much time you actually devote to singing. Some dancers have a fascination with the vocal learning process, and some find it a chore. It's not that the latter don't like to sing. Usually they have a blast performing the musical numbers in shows and rely on performing eight times a week to strengthen their voices. It's between gigs where the daily vocal upkeep can slide. If you love to explore your voice, by all means expand your repertoire. If you fall into the latter group, avoid the panic of not being in vocal shape for an audition by devoting a small amount of time each day to maintaining your two basic audition songs.

3. Evaluate how much money you can spend on lessons and sheet music. Whatever you choose to present in an audition must be well prepared by working with a coach and easy for the audition pianist to read.

4. The song itself should neither be too obscure, too common, overly limited in range, or too long. Let's pick this apart.

   A. Too obscure: Your friend, a budding lyricist/composer, has written a good but rather atonal song that has never been published and you think it's a perfect audition piece. Big mistake. If I, as a casting person, have no idea how the song is supposed to sound, how can I judge you? Are those notes in a minor key or are you singing flat? It is far more professional to choose a song that is from a produced Broadway or Off-Broadway show than to force the casting person to guess its origin and contents.

   B. Too common: Some songs are sung by everybody and his brother. Not only do the casting people silently groan at hearing the same song over and over all day long, but it's difficult not to compare one performance against the other. Keep your ears open at auditions. If too many people are singing your song, it's time for a change.

   C. Limited in range: To emphasize a particular mood or character in a show, some songs are purposely written using only four or five notes. While these songs are terrific in context, they present you as a Johnny One-Note in an audition.

   D. Too long: No one wants to listen to you sing for five minutes. If your song is repetitive, sing the verse and chorus once through and call it a day. The casting people will ask if they want to hear more.

5. Relating to the song: Sometimes the temptation arises to choose a song strictly for the notes it shows off. If you could care less about what the lyrics are saying but love landing the money note, your performance of the song will be technical but emotionally dead. Don't be a show-off. Choose songs whose story or sentiment you believe so that you can deliver not just notes, but a believable performance. With the myriad of songs written over the years there is bound to be one that you connect with and that includes the money note, too.

Once you have chosen your songs, keep a clean, easy-to-read copy for auditions. Handing the audition pianist a thick songbook that he has to hold open with one hand or that tends to catapult off the piano is not a good idea. If the music pages are photocopied from the library, tape them together so that they can be easily spread across the front of the piano. Many people keep their music in a loose-leaf notebook, the pages encased in plastic for easy maneuverability and to avoid wear and tear.

While mastering your songs vocally, consider how much staging to incorporate when you perform at an audition. The bottom line is this: in most auditions you dance first and sing later. Since the casting people have already seen you move, they now want to hear you. Some musical directors emphatically request no movement, but if you don't receive this dictate, stay away from intricate dance steps. Practice a few small arm and hand gestures to emphasize certain lyrics at specific times and let them suffice. The more you execute extraneous movements, the more it will look like you are deflecting attention away from your vocal ability. If you are singing a song from a show you have previously performed, stay away from the original choreography. The casting people will have already noticed this credit on your resume and to give them the performance you did onstage is tacky. It looks like you have no imagination to do anything else with a song.

Acting

When the curtain goes up, if you are supposed to be a merry villager, you can't mope around like a stick-in-the-mud. Nor can you stretch a fake grin from ear to ear like the village idiot. The former is self-indulgent and disrespecting your job; the latter is inexperience. Whatever mood you are portraying, whether you have lines or not, you must relate it to the audience. All members of a cast are characters—all are actors. You may be among the "peas and carrots" crowd of reactors to a scene, but those "peas and carrots" had better come from an organic place to enhance the world onstage.

GRACIELA DANIELE: Although I wasn't aware of it, I was always putting acting into my dancing. I had it in my soul. I couldn't just dance without feeling something in my body and my face. So I was acting without realizing it.

Acting is an integral part of those Broadway shows that contain few words. Shows like *Contact* and *Fosse* would fall limp without the acting abilities of the performers, no matter how extraordinary the choreography. The sets, lights, and costumes help clue in the audience, but it is the acting that makes the story come to life.

ROBERT MONTANO: What a waste. One time I went back to see *Cats* after I had left the show, and I overheard this kid who was playing Mistoffelees say, "This show sucks. There's no acting involved." I thought to myself, "Wow. He's missing the boat." There is acting involved. So the show isn't Shakespeare, but you have to know the age and essence of each character. You have to know how to walk if you're Old Deuteronomy or have the frenetic energy of a kitten. It's your job as a dancer/actor to dig in to the character.

JIM BORSTELMANN: I'm a dancer who acts the heck out of every step. What a bore to watch someone do a high kick or a sharp flick just for the sake of doing it. There has to be a reason beyond that, a reason that supports the movement. Don't just stand up there and be pretty. That's boring. Dancers come in every shape and size, but when someone's doing the whole thing? That's what catches my eye.

Some performers attend an acting school and some study in private groups with an individual teacher. There are many good acting teachers around the country. As with voice teachers, check *Back Stage* and ask local theatres and colleges. Most New York acting schools recommend that you audit a class for a small sum. This is an excellent idea to see if you like the style of teaching and to see if you feel comfortable. Acting involves baring your emotions, so you don't want an atmosphere that is inhibiting. Auditing policies differ, so be sure to be informed, punctual, and have exact change on hand to pay for the class.

Take advantage of hands-on experiences. When you rehearse and perform a show, you are surrounded by directors, choreographers, and other actors who will guide you. Keep your eyes open to what you consider good acting and clue into the technique. It is rather ellusive because each show demands a different style, and each actor and director work differently, but the goal is the same: to create a believable character.

TOMMY TUNE: Because of my height I would start getting picked out of the chorus to do special things. I had been schooled in acting and all so when they had a couple of lines here and there that they would toss to the chorus, I would get them. One time I got beat out of a two-line thing and it turns out that it was by Christopher Walken. That's okay. He's such a fine actor, I get it.

If there are no acting classes available, don't let that stop you. Reading books on acting and memorizing monologues will help to initiate basic acting skills. The best favor you can do for yourself is to read plays out loud alone or with friends. Backyards, apartments, or garages all make viable arenas. My neighbors in Manhattan were fantastic about getting together to read scripts, much to my chagrin. My back window overlooked their courtyard and I would overhear juicy conversations of illicit affairs, financial takeovers, and murder. Admittedly my curiosity about these strange neighbors got the best of me, so I would hide beside the window to eavesdrop. Once when there was talk of torture and I saw their friend tied up I nearly called the cops until I suddenly recognized the dialogue. They were doing a scene from *Death and the Maiden*. Boy, was I a dope. I had been so obsessed with being a busybody I didn't realize that they met every week to read play scripts. What a credit to their diligence, and their acting.

LUIS PEREZ: We had a loose drama club in high school. It was just me and five buddies that liked to do theatre. We had an advisor in name only, because the teacher never came to any of the meetings. One afternoon a week the five of us would read through plays or put on a musical, doing huge shows with this teeny cast—stealing wood and building sets, costuming, everything. One year we entered in a state thespian competition with all the different schools around Florida. We won best mime, best duo for a play, best monologue. It was a clean sweep!

Because dancers don't need to talk out loud in developing their technique, you may not be aware that you have a regional accent. When I attended The Boston Conservatory, some of the kinder descriptions of my Worcester, Massachusetts, accent were, "nasal," "strident," and "way too loud." Add to that my placing the letter *r* where there was none, and never pronouncing those that did exist, I was a dialectic mess. It took me six months just to hear myself, another year to remove it, and half a year more to master other regional and foreign accents. The hard work especially paid off when I auditioned for the role of Grushinskya in Tommy Tune's *Grand Hotel.* I was told to read in either a French or Russian accent. I chose Russian, since I was more comfortable with it. For my callback, Tommy requested French, so I relearned the script. The happy result is that I was fortunate enough to play the role both on Broadway and on the national tour.

Some accents are colorful and some annoying, but either way, you should develop a Standard American style of speech. Merely saying your name in an audition will classify you for better or worse. If you are asked to read for a show that takes place in Brooklyn and your speech is limited to a Southern drawl, you won't get the part.

CHITA RIVERA: The only accent I recall that I had was a little Southern. I used to say "Y'all." But when I was in *West Side Story* in London, I fell in love with the word; the English language. I always loved hearing every word clearly. It would make me crazy when I couldn't hear the lyric of a song. It is the conversation—what you are trying to communicate. If I can't hear it, I don't know what you are talking about. You have to get those lyrics across. Otherwise, I'll just listen to the notes.

Attend a speech class or practice the tapes that accompany books such as *Stage Dialects* by Jerry Blunt. If you normally sound like one of the accents except Standard American, you've got some work to do. Once you get the hang of it, tape yourself and see if you can hear where your regionalisms sneak in. Don't worry that you may lose an accent that you might need someday. It will come back in a flash. Your pursuit is to be able to control it.

JoAnn M. Hunter: The performers from Opryland always made fun of the way I talked. I thought I spoke correctly and that they were the ones with the accent. Then one day we were talking about breakfast and I mentioned flipping pancakes with a spatuler. They asked, "With what?" and I repeated, "Spatuler," thinking they were just stupid hicks. One guy said, "Spatula," emphasizing the *a*. I was so humiliated, especially at the age of eighteen thinking that spatula ended in *er*. So I started taping myself. I would read any magazine out loud, tape myself, and listen to how I sounded. My God, it was like the worst of Boston and New York and me in the middle.

There are added benefits to perfecting your speech besides getting lines or a part on Broadway. To augment your finances, you may audition for television commercials, series, daytime dramas, voice-overs, or film. Listen to the typical voices on television, both performers and newscasters alike. There is no noticeable accent, unless the character is specifically defined. Being able to drop your regionalism or add a different one may earn you a tidy chunk of change.

Performance Onstage

Some teachers think that performing in recitals, presentations, or community theatre takes away from focusing on technique. Indeed, some colleges won't let you perform until your junior or senior year. I believe that performing is necessary. It is the next level of growth. While the classroom is a place of discipline and self-improvement, it is also a place of choices. Your teacher may goad you to tears, but ultimately the choice is yours to improve, or not, at your own pace. Performing on a stage is the real deal, the deadline. If you haven't perfected your choreography or your song to the best of your ability, it's you and only you who will fail. This wonderful opportunity of meeting your performance deadline spurs you to nail that pirouette or hit that high note. Instead of taking time away from perfecting technique, you will be eager to spend even more time practicing.

Performing allows you to give yourself to the meaning of the moment and the movement while living in a magical world of accoutrements. The costumes, makeup, sets, and lights augment what you have so painstakingly learned. Your steps are no longer textbook dry, but transcend to character and emotion. There is no finer feeling, nor no better gift to the audience.

GRACIELA DANIELE: When I was eight years old at the Teatro Colón we had to take our dance classes and we also had to be the extras in everything. We were the little black children in *Aida* holding candles in the opera at night and then up at six the next morning to go to class. Then we would spend the entire morning in the theatre and in the afternoon I would go to my normal school. It was hard—a lot of work. But I loved it: the stories, the plots of the operas, the extraordinary music, the big orchestra, the opera and ballet stars coming in. It was like living inside an enchanting fairy tale plus having the physical challenge of the sport of dancing.

TOMMY TUNE: I went onstage so early. I don't think you can get enough experience on a stage. Yes, we're going for some kind of technical perfection in the room, but there's an experience that you get with performing that separates you from those who are simply technically trained. They are fabulous, but they can blend into the background. Like those people you see in class who are fabulous at the barre with their legs up to their ears, but when they come out onto the floor at an audition they don't have any sense of the choreographer's style or what he was trying to express. They give the perfect "thing" but they don't get the job. You need a healthy balance of both. The more you can perform wherever, the more experience you gain. Just give me a stage. I'll play anywhere. I would do it then, and I'll do it now. You need to express your soul, to have that physical dialogue with the audience. And that improves with repetition.

BEBE NEUWIRTH: I would get out of school a lot to perform at nursing homes, grammar schools, all over. One time it was in a tiny library and the wings were the stacks of books. Priceless education. Although I don't believe you can teach stage presence because it has to do with the energy of one's own being, I do believe that the more you perform, the more confident you become under those circumstances. The audience, the lights, the silence, everyone looking at you can terrify some people, but the more you do it, the easier it is to find your way around out there.

Feeling at home onstage is terribly important because the more comfortable you feel, the more you can think clearly. This concept hit me rather early in life when my sister and I were performing at a home for the mentally handicapped. In the middle of our tap routine, a woman climbed onto the stage, lifted her skirt, and peed. Without saying a word to each other, we tip-tapped our way to the other end of the stage while a nurse led the smiling woman away. The challenge for the rest of the number was to avoid the puddle. Had we not had extensive performing experience at recitals, nursing homes, minstrel shows, and reform schools, we probably would have panicked and bolted for the wings.

JULIO MONGE: From early on in Puerto Rico I was so involved with all the different areas of theatre and really doing it, earning a living. So by the time I got to New York, even though it was not so sharp yet, I knew performing. Which is the key.

LUIS PEREZ: *Unsinkable Molly Brown* was my first dinner theatre gig. I was fifteen years old. I'd stay there and help paint and build the sets. It was the coolest. I was paid ten dollars a show. That was probably my most rewarding pay. And, of course, I got the free trout dinner.

Performing can curb the tendency of being blindly self-involved and helps develop skills that have nothing to do with natural ability; skills that will make you a valuable professional. Of course, choreographers appreciate the "gifted" performer who catches their eye, but a stage-full of gifts who are not used to the stage can be an assault to the eye, the choreography, and to the production. Consider what you will learn by often being onstage:

1. Recognizing light sources is imperative. You will feel the hot spots, the cold spots, and be aware of either being in, or not blocking, side lighting. When it is your moment, you don't want to dance in the dark, nor do you want to cast shadows on fellow performers.
2. Hearing clearly lets you gauge audience reaction. Many cues are taken "when the applause peaks," "just as the applause fades,"

"after the laugh," or "if there is no laugh." Another cue may be "when you hear so-and-so on stage left take a breath." Hearing clearly also keeps you abreast of unforeseen circumstances that have nothing to do with the normal action of the show. A piece of the set may be falling in your direction, another dancer may get injured or ill, or someone in the audience may have a heart attack. Although you keep performing, you will be able to keep an ear out to adjust staging or hear the stage management call a halt to the show.

3. Orchestra conductors and musicians are as fallible as anyone else. After all, one of the delightful aspects of theatre is that it is live. An experienced performer can adjust to unexpected tempo changes, missing bars of music, and early or late cues. When the music seems impossibly fast or excruciatingly slow, you will be able to suck it up and change without the audience knowing. Even when the music is canned, ghostly things can happen to the tape.

4. Many performers experience jitters before going on, but time onstage teaches you to control the nerves. You learn to focus your energy, even when it is the first public performance. Many inexperienced performers are fine in the rehearsal room, but completely blank out with stage fright. The most annoying greenhorns turn into cyclones onstage. They can unintentionally steal stage space, kick other dancers, jump on laugh lines, or not keep moving when they hit the wings when leading a chorus line offstage. This inexperience shrouds any respect you have gained from your fellow performers.

5. One of the most invigorating, yet demanding, aspects of theatre is that once you get into previews you are a public work in progress. Enormous changes in the choreography may be made during daytime rehearsals. Sometimes an entirely new number goes into the show that very evening. Onstage experience allows you to deliver an acceptable performance even though your mind is racing to remember the new steps, new lyrics, and new entrances and exits.

6. In the unfortunate event that another performer is injured, you must be able to adapt in a flash. Many times the dance captain won't have the opportunity to tell you exactly what to do to adjust spacing or to dance alone if it's your partner who went down. Perhaps the injured person's job was to execute an important piece of stage business like moving a chair, delivering a prop from one side

of the stage to the other, or lifting the star of the show. If you are aware, you can be of immense help in picking up the slack. The more comfortable you are in your stage world, the more you can use your common sense to patch all sorts of problems.

7. The transition from the studio to the stage is a transition from the simple world of tights, leotards, and fake props to a world chock full of costumes, wigs, makeup, props, quick-change booths, television monitors, microphones, tracked floor surfaces, raked stages, passarelles, treadmills, turntables, staircases, cross-overs and crossunders, computerized sets, blocked sightlines, and, above all, a pressing time clock. Every stage, and every show mounted on every stage, is different. No matter how meticulously the director and choreographer preplan the move to the theatre, there are always unique quirks. The more you can solve your own problems and organize your stage business, the more the director and choreographer can address the big snafus. This comes with experience. You can't solve a problem if you don't recognize it in the first place.

JoANN M. HUNTER: When I was growing up my dance teacher gave me so many opportunities to perform—recitals, competitions at Dance Masters of America—wherever she could get us out. Later I worked at Opryland for two years. It was a great experience. I learned to perform, I learned continuity, I learned how to do four or five shows a day, six days a week, and keep it fresh. You do a dance recital once a year—big deal. I was doing the same choreography over and over and trying to keep it fresh. It was my first exposure to that. I will probably never work that hard again, but for someone young, it's a great thing to do.

As I mentioned earlier, when you are onstage, the stakes are heightened. Each show is a one-shot deal for both you and the audience. Consequently, the stage is a pitiless master. The moment you step out of the wings, you belong to that other world. There are no bathroom breaks, no excuses, and there's no turning back. What you have started you must finish, come hell or high water. Many times you discover a well of courage and untapped capabilities in the heat of the moment, especially concerning pain. In a classroom we all have the normal hurts—stretching, cramping, shin splints. If we suffer a serious injury, we limp to the side and call for an ice pack. Onstage a serious injury can occur and somehow we summon up the ability to continue performing.

Here is a personal example of the power of performance. Graciela Daniele's Off-Broadway production of *Tango Apasionado* was an extraordinary show, but a bear to dance. Not only did it include intricate Tango, but intense acting, knife fights, and rape. In one sequence, I underwent a violent, simulated rape by two men, at the end of which I was shoved off a table, over a chair, and onto the floor. One evening as I hit the floor, I felt a sickening rotation in my shoulder. The offstage cast was horrified to see that I suddenly turned into a camisole-clad Quasimodo due to a dislocated shoulder. Something—adrenaline, spirit, commitment—kept me going through to the end of the show. The audience never noticed. This postponement of pain is, to me, a testament of the power of the mind, and the stage.

CHITA RIVERA: Something happened to everybody in *Can-Can* because it was a very athletic show. One night, doing a cartwheel section, my calf and thigh went in opposite directions, injuring my knee. I felt it go, but then I had an exit. I hit stage right and my leg just collapsed. Reality smacked me in the face, but I had to get back onstage so I went, "Five, six, seven, eight . . ." and made my reentrance. That's what we do. And it's an interesting lesson because if you have the right training, you learn that there's a lot more you can do than you think you can do. I don't accept complaining or missing shows because you sneeze. You have to challenge yourself.

Performance Offstage

Your performance is not strictly limited to the stage. In an audition no matter how nervous or ill you are feeling, no matter how much you hate the choreography, no matter how much you want to scream when you are rejected, no matter how much you abhor the dancer standing next to you, don't let it show. Not in the studio, not in the hallways or bathrooms, not anywhere you can be seen or heard by someone connected to the production, or for that matter, connected to any other production that happens to be auditioning or rehearsing in the same space. The theatre is a very small world with very big ears. This rule also applies when you are in class or rehearsal. News of good or bad reputations telegraphs through the theatre community faster than Western Union.

Once you land a show, no matter if it's on Broadway or in the smallest regional theatre, you represent the show. As you exit the stage door, fans will want to gape at you, sometimes gathering the nerve to ask for an autograph. Courtesy and a simple smile is all you need to give them if you don't want to spend a lot of time. For the show's publicity, you may be asked to appear on television shows or give newspaper interviews. Don't dress like a pig, and mind your manners in these professional engagements. Whatever the situation, your offstage performance will be appreciated by your producers and will classify you as a true professional.

Dancer/Singer/Actor. There is an old saying that bad news comes in threes. On Broadway, just the opposite is true. The triple threat is a casting director's dream. If you find the time to add words and song to your dancing, you will never regret it.

LUIS PEREZ: Coming from being a principal in the Joffrey to Bernardo in *West Side Story*, I was a sheet of solid muscle and technique. I couldn't understand why the guys were getting tired doing things that to me were a walk in the park. I didn't have the wherewithal to realize that they had so much that I lacked. They were triple threats. A lot of them were better-trained actors than me and all were better singers. Yes, I was probably the most gifted dancer, but that isn't the only aspect of a musical.

CHAPTER FIVE

College or Not: The Toss-up

Now that you have a handle on what kinds of teachers, techniques, and talents are valuable to develop, you must choose which particular route to Broadway is right for you. Will a dance college offer you an inspiring curriculum? Do you come directly to New York? Should you first follow your interest in pure dance by joining a dance company? It's a tough call. No fortune-teller can predict your success in the theatre because it is entirely dependent upon your talent, timing, the atmosphere of theatre during certain years, and a little bit of luck. If you take the four years to go to college, you may miss a boon period for shows that need young dancers. If you take your time in school or in a dance company, you may come to New York better prepared to handle a variety of shows.

The reality is that there is a time constriction for dancers. Your body will age, your personal life will become more complicated, and although there are shows that have an older dancing chorus, the majority are for performers from eighteen years old to the early forties. Arriving in New York at twenty-three, unless you are going for a ballet company, certainly doesn't put you over the hill. You are still on the younger side of prime age.

Perhaps this will be the first time you will be living away from home. As old and wise as you may feel at eighteen, you still have a lot to learn about managing your life. New York is a wonderful place but it is fast and unforgiving if you don't immediately land a job. A few years of scraping to pay the rent, rejection in auditions, smoldering summer subways, and walking the streets with guarded, sometimes angry, sometimes truly weird people can frustrate you and your career. In your heart, you've got to be ready for the move. Some people are driven to come to New York right away from high school, but if you have any hesitation, it's perfectly fine to bide your time.

Let's look at the pros and cons of five routes: going to college, coming directly to New York without going to college, coming to New York to attend one of the city's colleges or music schools, working in LORT theatres (League of Resident Theatres), or joining a dance company. Last, I include two alternate routes.

College

A good college or conservatory offers you many styles of dance, as well as acting, speech, music, and theatre craft courses. Although the dance, musical theatre, and music departments may be separated, they usually are not exclusive. For a yearly tuition you receive a well-rounded education in technique, the histories and theories of art, music, dance, and drama, and the required academics for a bachelor's degree. Some colleges have majors in ballet or modern, and some lean more toward concert dance than musical theatre. This is something you should check carefully before deciding to attend.

No matter the curriculum, a working knowledge and respect for all aspects of theatre is developed. You may perform in one concert, build the sets for another, create costumes for another, and run the lights and sound for yet another. The drudge work—mopping the stage or dusting the costume room—may also be part of the requirements. If you are in the dance department, you will not receive extensive dramatic training, and vice versa, but you will certainly get a healthy taste of each. Certain colleges agree to let you take extra classes that interest you in another department.

I am extremely thankful for the education I received at The Boston Conservatory. Although I was a good jazz and tap dancer at seventeen, I was not proficient in ballet and modern. As a matter of fact, I assumed modern was disco dancing! The intense curriculum molded my technique and opened my mind and body to accomplish what I never dreamed I could do. Because I was so hungry to improve, the teachers allowed me to take as many extra dance classes as I wanted. Quite often I literally danced from eight in the morning to nine at night seven days a week, taking classes, rehearsing workshops, and performing in both the dance and theatre departments. During the summer I stayed at school for the summer dance program. What a miracle it seemed to me that in a few short years of hard work I blossomed from a jazz baby to a viable ballet, modern, and theatre dancer.

LUIS PEREZ: For theatre, I am jealous of people who went to schools like The Boston Conservatory, Northwestern University, Juilliard, or Carnegie Mellon because everyone who comes out of there has an amazing ability and an amazing amount of talent. There are certain things they don't know by not coming up through the ranks, but they always come in self-assured. Unless you are a miracle freak of nature, I think the college system is great if you can get into the right college. Of course, I also know a lot of great people who didn't go to college. But if I had it to do over, and I was not aiming for ballet, I'd probably have gone to college.

Another plus about a dance college or conservatory is that you will learn to teach dance and will be required to choreograph—in other words, you will be forced to the "other side" (not to be confused with Darth Vader's "dark side"). As a performer you may buck these requirements, or you may find that you enjoy them. Whatever your inclination, the invaluable truth is that you learn a great deal about technique, design, your method of creation, and your barometer of patience in molding someone other than yourself. Opportunities like this are extremely rare in New York, unless you have the credits to teach or, to choreograph, can pay a group of dancers to work with you.

By teaching and choreographing, when you are working with professional choreographers on shows, you will understand why they may happen to put their heads in their hands or call an unscheduled five-minute break. You may not be privy to the details of the frustration, but you will wisely know to keep your mouth shut until they come back ready to work. When they do, you will know to execute what they ask 100 percent without question. This understanding is worth its weight in gold.

TOMMY TUNE: I'm not sorry that I took the extra years to go to college. It opened my eyes to so much more, even though I may not have understood it at the moment. What was taught in the art appreciation, theatre history, and directing classes I still carry with me. All of this knowledge flows into the same creative river. Maybe this little bit more intelligence was picked up by the directors or choreographers who hired me, besides the fact that I could technically do what they needed. Maybe I brought more to the stage.

Parents will hate me for saying this, but there's one thing about college that is undeniable: you can always drop out.

DAVID WARREN-GIBSON: I took three years of college—arts and literature. Then I convinced my parents to let me go to New York just to try it out. I stayed in a friend of a friend of a friend's apartment on Sullivan Street, one of the basement kind with the roaches. I thought I'd moved to hell. I was used to this suburban, sunshine life with lawns and here I was in a dark hell in New York City in February! I got really sad, really upset, so I went back to Houston. After another year of college I came back and finally stayed when I was twenty-two.

JULIO MONGE: I figured I would come to New York when I finished college. But Frank Hatchett from the Broadway Dance Center brought a Broadway Dance Caravan to Puerto Rico with Gus Giordano and some ballet people. Somehow I was in the front of the class and Frank said, "Come over here." I thought it was because I had a red leotard on. Bright red. How wrong is that? But he used me as his assistant to demonstrate. After the class, he and Gus offered me a scholarship to either go to Chicago or New York. Everything changed right then. Chicago— hmmm, New York—yeah! I went to New York that summer with two suitcases and two hundred dollars in my pocket. Since then I've been blessed to have worked with people at such a high level—Jerome Robbins, Vanessa Redgrave, Paul Simon . . . What they have gets into your bones just watching, listening, both in rehearsal and in the wings. You don't get that in a school.

LUIS PEREZ: My father saw me getting more and more into ballet as I got older, and he wasn't pleased that I wanted to go the Joffrey instead of finishing college. I was supposed to be a doctor. I was already in college at sixteen, so my mother proposed a deal. She said, "Look, Luis is two years ahead of his class, so let's make a deal with him. If he makes dean's list this year in all maths and sciences, let's give him a year or two in New

York." My father sat me down and asked, "Do you really want to do this? What happens if you get into a ballet company, but you are the corps boy in the back?" I said, "That will never happen. I'll work myself to death to not let that happen." By the time I was twenty-one I was a principal in the Joffrey and spent the next seven years there. When I visited him just before he died, his first words were, "How did you dance?" He was proud.

MAMIE DUNCAN-GIBBS: Trying to pay for college on my own was such a struggle. I took out a student loan and I had a couple of grants, but I was always so miserable and so broke and around kids whose parents had paid for school by writing a check the first day. It was also during a bad prejudice time in Boston. Not so much in the school, but my roommate did accuse me of stealing her money because I'm black and "all black people steal." She actually said that! That one year was so hard I thought, "I can't go through three more years of this." My mother said, "Pray about it. The Lord will provide." And I remember thinking, "Jesus Christ! That's good for you but that's not working for me right now!"

You might even make a deal with your parents that the money they would have spent on all four years of college is saved for when you want to establish yourself in New York.

BEBE NEUWIRTH: My parents gave me a brilliant and sensitive gift. It had to do with their focus on education and their focus on fairness as well. I was attending Juilliard, but I was very unhappy. My focus was on musical theatre and the curriculum at that time was geared more toward concert dance. My parents said, "Okay, we have saved to make sure that you and your brother would have enough money for a college education. Make your own school. Find all the classes you want to take and we will support you." I did just that. I left Juilliard, arranged my own classes, and slightly less than a year later I got my first job in *A Chorus Line*. Now I tease them that they owe me two more years of school.

Whatever college you choose, see if you qualify for a scholarship. Once I paid for my first semester, I went on academic scholarship for the remaining three and a half years. Others received dance scholarships. With the academic scholarship, I only had to keep my grades up. Those on dance scholarship had to perform duties to maintain the cleanliness of the school. Each college has its own policies and qualifications, but no matter the requirements, they are well worth it.

The snag to a college education is that your degree doesn't mean squat in an audition. A doctor goes to medical school and earns a grade point average that determines which hospital will accept her for internship and residency. After that she can set up shop. Or a high school teacher studies through grad school, passes the certification exam, and secures a teaching position. These are wonderful professions, but the salaried appointments largely depend on the paperwork, the grades, the degree. Not so in theatre. No one cares about the degree, except as a barometer to the amount of training you've had. They care if a dancer can do the arabesque, the jump, the turn. That's what gets you the job.

New York—No College

If you come to New York directly from high school and wish to study the entire curriculum offered under a college's one roof, you'd better be independently wealthy. To take that many classes, you would not have time for a part-time job or the travel time from uptown to down. On the other hand, the teachers in New York are fabulous and numerous, you are surrounded by professionals who are actively working their craft, and you are available to audition for the jobs that will carve your career. There is no better teacher than experience and educating yourself because you love it.

GRACIELA DANIELE: One time I was talking with Joe Papp and I said that I sometimes feel very shy because everybody here has graduated this and that, and I don't have that. He said, "What are you talking about? In college people learn what is given to them. You learned what was important to you. You read yourself. How many languages do you speak?" I said, "Well, four." He said, "Did you read Aristotle?" I said, "Yes, of course. I bought Aristotle and I didn't like it too much. I don't agree with his ideas about women." And he laughed and said, "You have a mind of your own. You have a universal education that Americans don't have. So why should you feel badly?" But inside it's still intimidating when someone has gone to Yale and I only have a high school diploma. But it's funny. Now as I go to speak at Yale or other colleges, I always start by saying that I have no academic credits, but I have experience. Experience.

MICHAEL KUBALA: New York University accepted me for a summer dance workshop when I graduated high school. I went with my clothes, five hundred dollars, and my bed. For me, the workshop was a kind of a trial-and-error type of thing to see if I liked it, if I fit in, and to earn a couple of credits. When you graduate the course, you sit in front of a board and they ask you about your future, what you want to do, and so on. Rachel Lampert was the director at that time and she said, "You could work on Broadway right now if you wanted to." They offered me a three-year scholarship after the first year. So I asked my mom for the money for the first year, but she didn't have it. I realized nothing was going to happen with no bucks for school. So I stayed in New York, got a job as a waiter, and went on scholarship at Ronn Forella's studio. I got my first Broadway show when I was twenty.

EUGENE FLEMING: After the summer at the School of American Ballet I went back to the North Carolina School of the Arts to start college, but in the first week I got a call from *A Chorus Line* offering me a job. I went to talk to the dean of dance and he said, "This is what you are training for. I won't tell you not to take a job because if it came my way, I would take it. For all the kids here, we hope that after four years they are able to get a job. Right now you have what they are working toward."

Coming to New York on your own can be more terrifying for your parents than for you. Although the city has cleaned up, it is still big, fast, expensive, and lures all types of people. If you have friends here, you have a big advantage. They can help you find your way around town and can fill you in on street sense. Knowing how to walk so you don't look like a tourist, judging how long to look someone in the eye, timing when to cross streets to avoid cab-crazy traffic or to bypass a lunatic without drawing attention, and never playing those pea-under-the-shell scams are mere fractions of the uncanny street savvy New Yorkers use daily. When you live here, this unwritten knowledge will seep into your pores, but having a friendly guide helps.

Point zero is that you need a place to live and money. In Chapter 6 I detail the options. Whatever career route brings you to New York, the basics are the same: You need to work to support yourself, in theatre or out; you want to keep advancing your dance, singing, and acting technique; you must audition, audition, audition.

Before jumping on a plane, thoroughly investigate what shows are currently running and what shows are coming up. If 90 percent of the musicals call for older dancers or pure singers, it might be wise to wait until the environment changes if you are hoping to immediately land a Broadway show. However, if you see that *Music Man*, *42nd Street*, and *Fosse* are playing, your chances of getting a job increase. If you don't get the Broadway gig, you might get the national tour.

Keeping up to date with pre-Broadway workshops, tours, and productions mounted at LORT theatres whose goal is to bring a particular show in, is a barometer for your prospects. Learn who is choreographing or directing what. Certain choreographers include lots of dance, certain directors love dance, and certain directors hate it. Their past shows are a rather reliable indication of their styles.

Check if the audition breakdown lists a choreographer or says, "Musical Staging by . . ." In many cases, musical staging is for a show employing singers who move, and perhaps a few dancers. The movement is more character driven, and unless the script calls for a nineteen-year-old, the few dance jobs usually go to an older, more experienced person.

All of this information can be found daily or weekly online. Such websites as www.actorsequity.org, www.backstage.com, www.playbill.com, and www.broadway.com buzz with the latest auditions, projects, and gossip. Consider an online subscription to www.backstage.com for more detailed reports. As long as you realize that the chat rooms in many of these sites spread personal opinions as well as bona fide news, you should learn quite a bit.

By coming to New York directly from high school, you may deal with more rejection on Broadway, but the many other performing venues available will season you. Radio City Music Hall has auditions both for the Rockettes and for their seasonal shows and tours. Most dinner theatres, regional theatres, cruise lines, and theme parks audition in the city. It could be that the week you get here, you land a job taking you out of town for the next three months. That's okay. Learning to walk the walk and talk the talk in the midst of theatrical traffic is priceless.

My only caution about diving into the New York theatre scene at a young age is to not get jaded. Don't act older than you are, nor be so smart after one job you seem unable to continue learning. Your innocence, integrity, and endurance are your passports.

New York—College

A way to get the best of both worlds is to attend one of the colleges or universities in New York. The environment is safer, you will be among students from all over the country away from home for the first time, and housing is available and more affordable. While getting a superb education, you will be in the hub of the action. If you have time, you can take classes at the many studios, depending on the school's policy. There is no risk in going to a few auditions to test the waters, whether you take the job or not. And the exposure to museums, concerts, dance, theatre—Broadway, Off-Broadway, Off-Off, uptown, downtown, east and west—is unsurpassed, many times at a student discount. Getting accepted to a New York institution may not be easy and it might cost a pretty penny, but this is a very smart route to take.

BEBE NEUWIRTH: I didn't know that there was anyplace to go other than New York City if you wanted to become a professional so I auditioned for Juilliard and Purchase and got accepted by both. I chose Juilliard so that I could be right in the city and could start auditioning for musical theatre, take jazz class, and learn how to sing.

Since Broadway casting directors, directors, and choreographers live in New York, they go to see student productions at the performing arts schools more often than their scheduled visits elsewhere. By participating simply as a part of your curriculum, you are gaining exposure. It is unlikely that they will run up to you, begging you to be in their next production, but you may pique their interest for the future. You are here. Casting directors and agents can keep an eye on your progress, and in auditions, choreographers and directors may recognize you.

Working in LORT Theatres

Productions from established theatres such as the Goodman in Chicago, the La Jolla Playhouse and the Old Globe in San Diego, A.C.T. in San Francisco, the Alley in Houston, the Mark Taper Forum in Los Angeles, and the Hartford Stage Company sometimes develop and bring their productions into New York. Depending on the producers, local talent may come in with the production. Within New York, anything done at

Lincoln Center is on a LORT contract, but many productions are considered Broadway shows. While I don't suggest waiting in your hometown for the chance of a show moving, I do recommend attending auditions in New York for productions that are developed at large-scale LORT theatres. If the show comes in, as in the case of *Hairspray, The Full Monty, Tommy, How to Succeed in Business, Jelly's Last Jam,* and *Thoroughly Modern Millie,* you will be on Broadway where the theatre community can view your work. What a terrific opportunity.

Dance Companies

Whether they went to college or not, many, many Broadway dancers were members of dance companies. Their success on Broadway proves that age is not a factor. Personally, this was the route I took—after graduating from college I spent three years in France with Les Ballets de Marseille de Roland Petit and then made a final move to New York. Even at that, I danced in two modern dance companies before switching to Broadway. Then I took two national tours, *Hello, Dolly!* and *A Chorus Line,* before landing my first show on Broadway. I was twenty-seven years old and, with all humility, a dancing whiz from all the experience I gained en route.

JIM BORSTELMANN: I did a year with Buffalo Ballet Theatre. It's crazy—a kid who grows up right next door to New York goes to Buffalo to learn to train. Kids from Buffalo would kill to come here. Well, I went there!

A dance company gives you a family—a secure environment away from home. The opportunities to perfect your technique come with company class, rehearsals, and performances. You may learn several styles of dance from different ballet masters and choreographers, or you may hone in on one choreographer's method. A dancer is the company's investment; it is to their advantage if you improve. Such attention may not come from an independent studio where you pay them for instruction, or even from a college.

I have only two cautions with a dance company. First, if it is too insular, you may lose sight of your dream amidst company politics. If you feel yourself drying out artistically or disparaging your own talent, it's time to look yourself in the mirror and ask, "Is this what I really want?"

The qualities you have that may be less than ideal for a particular company may be the exact qualities that are enviable in another arena.

The second caution is that developing your acting and singing abilities will not only take second place, they may be mocked. In the opinion of many so-called serious dancers, Broadway is to art what the immigrant class was to the highbrows on the *Titanic*—low-class, cheap, and vulgar. Who cares about such prejudicial snobbery? Jerome Robbins, George Balanchine, Agnes DeMille, Michael Kidd, Catherine Dunham, Lars Lubovitch, Garth Fagan, John Caraffa, and Mark Dendy, among many other concert dance choreographers, have worked on Broadway. Gee, I guess they're low class, too. Dismiss the narrow-minded scaredy-cats and get on with all that inspires you.

Alternate Routes

There are two other ways to get a Broadway show without making the ultimate decision to move to New York: spending a limited time in New York or auditioning for a national tour when it comes to your vicinity.

Depending on your accessibility to the city, you can travel in strictly to audition for a particular show. Of course, taking the PATH train from New Jersey is a lot easier than the red-eye from California, but if you have the money and a place to stay, you could spend a day, a week, or if you've got generous friends who don't mind your sharing their bathroom, an entire summer. Approach the trip as you would a slot machine—there are no guarantees you will hit the jackpot. Be aware that all shows have callbacks so if you pass the first audition, you will have to return. The callbacks could be in the same week, or may not be until a month or so later. Figure this into your financial picture. What a shame it would be if you aced the first audition and couldn't return.

The national tours of some Broadway shows hold auditions in the cities they visit. Although they leave New York with complete casts, their numbers can dwindle for a variety of reasons. Injuries can be the culprit, some people get tired of being on the road, and, if the show is still running on Broadway, some are called in to join the Broadway cast. When a show comes into town, ask if they will be holding auditions. If you get the job, you will tour with the company and collect a high salary with per diem doing a job you love. If you are lucky, you might get switched into New York. At the least, which in reality is quite a bit, you will be performing with true professionals and meeting the creators when they come out to clean up the show. A national tour is the next best thing to Broadway on your resume.

How and when to come to Broadway are personal choices. We are all individuals with unique circumstances and concerns. The cliché is absolutely true that you must follow your heart. Remember that when you are eighteen into your twenties you are unstoppable. This is the time of your life when the world can be conquered without thought to the personal constraints that may mount as you get older—you have the invincible tunnel vision of youth. Whatever your choice, grab each adventure with total commitment and you can't go wrong. You'll know when the time is ripe.

CAITLIN CARTER: A lot of kids in the ballet department didn't care about college at the North Carolina School of the Arts, but I applied to colleges my senior year just in case I decided to go. I got accepted to Stanford, University of California at Berkeley, Rice, Grinnell, but I deferred for two years. I told my dad, "Let me see if I can do this—work as a dancer." I was in two different ballet companies over the two years, but I was angsting about staying in ballet. One company was going to fold and I'd have to start auditioning all over again. I knew I was good, but not great. I wouldn't get into ABT or anything like that, I wouldn't be a soloist, I'd be corps for the rest of my life. So I decided to go to college—Rice—and call it quits. Originally I was an economics major. Even though I did well, economics sucked. So boring. I missed dance so I started taking some classes around town and joined a jazz dance company. I stuck out all four years of college, switching to a double major of English and Art History, and then spent another year in Houston, doing theatre, modeling, commercials, industrials, and tours. I had all this going, but it's hard to make a living. On the other hand, I got connected with Broadway choreographers like Susan Stroman and Rob Marshall at Theatre Under the Stars and worked for Ann Reinking in Los Angeles. They helped me so much when I decided to try for Broadway. That might not have happened had I come to New York right away.

CHAPTER SIX

How Do I Pay For All This? The Cold Hard Facts and Cash

Looking back, I don't know how the hell I did it.
— Michael Kubala

A person entering college for a nontheatrical career has to consider tuition, room and board, books, personal items, and miscellaneous fees for a nine-month period over four years. As of 2002, Harvard University estimates the costs at $40,850 per school year. Other colleges and universities including Yale, Northwestern, and Penn State range from $21,000 for only tuition, room, and board, to $44,960 for a full-year program, extras included. These figures are based on a full-paying, out-of-state student.

Your costs in New York City will include dance classes, dance shoes and clothes, voice lessons, acting lessons, pictures, resumes, apartment, transportation, books, CDs, sheet music, theatre admissions, laundry, haircuts, toiletries, medical bills, and maybe a little food . . .

Broken down, the approximate figures are in the following table. Caveat! The prices in New York know one direction only—up.

Rent	$700–$2500 per month, depending on location; divide amount by number of roommates
Dance classes	$10–$13 per class
Dance clothes	$10.50–$21 tights $28–$40 jazz pants $16–$36 leotards $12–$23 leg warmers $14.50–$24 undergarments $30–$75 dancebag
Dance shoes	$16–$39 ballet $33–$89 jazz $51–$103 tap (with taps)
Voice lessons	$60–$75 per lesson
Acting lessons	$25–$50 per class; class sessions from five classes to full semester
Pictures	$99–$600 and up
Resumes	Basically free if you type it yourself
Picture copying	$16 for the negative; $65 per 100 copies; more if you want a border and your name
Resume copying	About seven cents a page; $7–$9 extra if they cut it to 8 × 10 size
Transportation	$2.00 one-way subway/bus fare
Books, scripts	$10–$25 each
CDs	$8.99–$31.99
Sheet music	$3.95–$5.95 each; compilations and scores: $10.95–$75
Theatre admission	$45–$100
Laundry	$15 per week
Haircut	$15–$50 and up
Toiletries, makeup	$30 per month
Food	$70 per week

Not included in the above list are security deposits, utilities, furniture, an answering machine or service, telephone and cable service, medical and dental bills, CD/tape player, a small tape recorder, everyday clothes and shoes, and all the miscellaneous items like dish detergent, toilet paper, and cockroach killer.

Let's say you take two dance classes a day, six days a week for most of the year, one weekly voice and acting lesson, and see theatre twice a month at a discount rate. We'll assume you buy a mere two sets of tights and leotards, that your shoes hardly wear out, and that you don't let your hair grow to Neanderthal length. Averaging all your other costs, your bare-bones yearly nut will be $35,529, if you live alone and never have a sore throat or a cavity.

How different is this from going to Harvard? There is one big difference. Paying for college is a one-time chunk of change, whereas our training never ends. After college and graduate school, most professions offer a tidy salary, basically guaranteed until retirement. We may earn a hefty salary on one job and subway fare on the next, when there *is* a next job. Living expenses are a necessity for all occupations, but staying in peak physical condition, constantly auditioning, and exposing yourself to all of the fine arts are essentials in ours. (If our profession isn't a real job, I don't know what is. Please.)

How can you afford all of these expenses to dance in New York City? The financial facts are sobering, yes; impossible, no. Some lucky people have parents who swing for everything, but the majority has to figure it out on their own.

CAITLIN CARTER: My father paid for everything: college, nice apartment, car. I had it easy my whole life. I really did. When I graduated, I told him I didn't want his support anymore. He freaked—said I didn't have to do that. But I wanted to make my own way.

EUGENE FLEMING: Coming right from high school and going into *A Chorus Line*, I didn't suffer for my art like some people had to do. On that note, I was blessed.

Support Jobs

Until you get a show that is lucrative either in town or on the road, you will need some kind of a job to support yourself. The contributing performers in this book have had myriad nontheatrical support jobs: receptionists; waiters in coffee shops, pancake houses, nightclubs, truck stops, delis, pizza parlors, cafés, upscale restaurants, catering, and as soda jerks and short-order cooks; paper and garment factory workers; models for clothing and art students; street mimes; house painters; ballroom teachers; temps; grocery clerks; baby-sitters; retail sales clerks; hotel cashiers; booksellers; health club instructors; go-go girls; coat checkers; and ice-cream scoopers. If it pays the bills, you do it.

Much to my credit or my chagrin, I worked a baker's dozen of the above jobs. Some were pretty horrendous. Working as a go-go dancer (back when go-go dancers wore bathing suits) was okay except for the solicitations from pimps and drug dealers and the policy of twenty on, twenty off. (You had to dance for twenty minutes then hustle drinks for the next twenty, totaling at least ten drinks throughout the night or you were fired. Being a greenhorn, I didn't know to tell the bartender to water my drinks. My morning ballet class was a blur until I wised up.) Coffee shops were cool, except for the small tips and the "regulars" like the man who wept every time he ordered, or the toothless woman who would eat oatmeal and fried eggs with her hands. So gross. Being a coat-check girl was okay except in winter when I had to hang the coats on an overhead bar. Man, they got heavy!

DAVID WARREN-GIBSON: I had been with a large modeling agency in Houston, so when I came to New York they sent me out on some calls. I hated it. It was a rat race. I'd walk in a room with my little book and my little pictures and there would be twenty-five guys who all looked like Adonis. I just felt like a piece of meat. It's impersonal—a rough world. They will talk about you right in front of you, like there's nothing going on inside of you. It's only, "What am I going to do with that hair, that pimple . . ." Like you're a third party.

MAMIE DUNCAN-GIBBS: I worked at a grocery store and then a health club. One day I came in and saw that they were offering jazz classes. I asked who was teaching and this little creep supervisor said that I was. I told him, "Not for two dollars and fifty cents I'm not." He said, "You'll do what I tell you." I said, "I will not," so he fired me. At least I got to collect unemployment.

JIM BORSTELMANN: I worked at Häagen-Dazs scooping ice cream, I did catering at Harkness House when they had parties, and my parents would also help me out. I'd eat scones for a dollar and a slice of Vinnie's pizza for dessert. More catering—Tavern on the Green. That was enough. I had money. You never think you're going to get old, responsible, and have to pay rent.

If you are going to put the time in, the more money you make, the better. As a waiter, places that serve liquor earn you bigger tips.

MICHAEL KUBALA: When I decided to stay in New York my roommate said, "I'm taking you up and down Third Avenue. We're getting you a job." So we went from restaurant to restaurant until I found Beau Geste, this place where two of the waiters were dancers. Even though I didn't know them, they told the owner that they knew me, I had worked at such and such restaurants, blah, blah. Bah-dah-boom. I got a job.

Being a temp can be lucrative if you are handy with computers, but it is a lot of sitting and the hours may not be convenient for taking class and auditioning. Look around until you find a situation that pleases you. No one says you have to stick with one job if you can earn money elsewhere, or if you absolutely hate it.

TOMMY TUNE: After I did *Irma La Douce* I came back to New York but it was winter and there wasn't much going on. I had enough money that I could just keep studying and going to auditions, but I didn't feel right about not working. So I got a job with an advertising agency. That was the only job-job I ever had. I only had it for a few weeks, but I received the only bonus I've ever gotten in my whole life. It was Christmastime and this wonderful company gave bonuses to everybody who was working for the company at the time.

JOANN M. HUNTER: I was down to my last twenty-four dollars in the bank and I had to pay my rent so I worked as a temp receptionist at a huge advertising agency. I didn't know how to use the switchboard so I hung up on so many people! When they'd call back I'd be so humiliated I'd disguise my voice. The firm offered me a permanent position there with benefits, a steady salary, you name it and I almost took it, thinking

I'd be set—no more worries. Then something went off in my head. This wasn't what I moved to New York for! So I turned it down.

Anytime you do a short-term show, industrial, commercial, film, soap, or extra work, you are eligible for unemployment if you have accrued enough weeks. In other words, you were not fired, but the employment ended. Let's say you quit your job at a restaurant in order to go on tour for ten weeks. You did not quit your last place of employment (the show), so you can receive unemployment benefits. Even a one-day commercial shoot is considered your last job. But before considering unemployment, beware of your base salary. If you work in a restaurant or drive a cab, your salary isn't very high since you work for tips. Unless your theatre jobs pay well, your combined income may not reflect a very high weekly unemployment rate. Still, temporary unemployment checks can be a blessing. Just be sure to let the unemployment office know that performing is your profession. They cannot offer you job opportunities in the theatre, but they can send you out to restaurants, offices, and the like if you admit to those nontheatrical skills as your primary profession. Keep a record of all the theatrical interviews or auditions you attend. You need to prove that you are seeking work, which of course, you are. You are a performer, not a mooch.

The positive side of working a support job is that you learn about life. Although many of your coworkers will be theatre hopefuls, you will meet all sorts of other characters. Observing their behavior is a great acting exercise. Budgeting your money, organizing your time, and handling yourself with decorum in awkward situations are all invaluable tools to help you grow as a person. You've heard it a million times that the definitive word in "Show Business" is "capital B—Business." The more experience you have in any type of business, the more prepared you will be for the knocks and negotiations in theatre.

Whatever you choose, remember you are in Manhattan to study and to find work in the theatre. Let your determination override your exhaustion and try to find a flexible employer, including yourself.

LUIS PEREZ: I didn't want to ask my parents for anything while I was on scholarship for the Joffrey. They were already helping with the rent. So I'd eat whatever, and to make extra money I'd perform mime in Washington Square Park. I really didn't know how to do mime—I just kind of imitated Marcel Marceau. The first night was pretty good. I made about a hundred bucks. The only problem is that I was so nervous about faking the performance I left my apartment keys at home. There I was late at night dressed all in black with these little white gloves and white makeup, climbing up the fire escape and into my window. A cat burglar in a top hat! People looked, but they didn't say anything. It was the Village.

Spend your money on your career training and save the rest. You will have to rethink what you consider a personal necessity. If it's a toss-up between that great sweater for $300 or new head shots, make the wise choice. If eating in lets you sock away next month's rent, forego the sit-down service in restaurants. Any money you save in the bank not only earns interest, but also future freedom.

Apartment

You've got to plan for a place to stay. A hotel is fine for a night or two, but the rates are extremely high. A weekend can set you back over $300. Hotels like the Chelsea Star Hotel have dormitory rooms for $29.99 per night or singles for $59, the YMCA on West 63rd is $64 per night with no bath, and companies like the Hospitality Company Inc. have furnished studio apartments for $675 per week. But multiply these rates over three months and you're talking serious money. If you have that much you can afford your own apartment.

If you are coming to New York to study with a particular school, find out if they have suggestions about where to stay. Ballet companies and colleges normally have good leads because they are entrusted with so many young people. However, if you plan on taking classes all around town, they probably can't help you. Living space is too limited and they would not have control of your whereabouts to make sure you pay the rent. It may be worth it to commit yourself to one of the larger schools for a summer. You would get the benefits of housing and intense training while you get the hang of living in New York.

Unless you have unlimited funds, you may not want to rush into an apartment situation. First of all, if you are not in NYC to view apartments, how do you know what you are really getting? Apartment hunting over the Web is convenient, but you won't know the reality of your home until you walk into it. Second, it is highly possible that soon after you come to New York, you'll get a job that takes you out of town. The choice is either to swallow the rent on an empty apartment or find someone to sublet. Third, if you have your own place, you have to furnish it. The furnishings can be meager, but the little costs can add up.

Friends, family, old dance teachers, and performers you have worked with are your best connections. They may have room themselves or know someone who needs a roommate, is subletting on a temporary basis, or is moving out out of town but wants to keep the apartment in town. Everyone in theatre is in the same boat as you: Rent is a struggle, when you least expect it you're employed out of town, and all had to find an initial place to stay. It is common to hop from apartment to apartment for years before getting your own place.

MAMIE DUNCAN-GIBBS: I lived with my sister on Long Island for four years, then I got a sublet on 29th Street. I could walk to class to save subway fare.

EUGENE FLEMING: When I came up to New York to go to SAB, my mother brought me to live with my aunt in Brooklyn. As soon as she got off the train she was like, "Whoop. Nope. Can't stay here. I'll pay you to come home." Then the mother of a girl I went to school with at North Carolina School of the Arts offered me a room in their apartment in Spanish Harlem. We went to check it out. My mom was a little leery on that one, but she let me stay.

TOMMY TUNE: When I finally got my own place, it was a basement apartment just like in *My Sister Eileen, Wonderful Town* where you just saw the feet walking by. Oh my God, I thought it was the greatest thing in the world. I made a vow: No matter how important or successful I become in this theatre business, I'm always going to live in this apartment. It cost seventy-five dollars a month and I figured I would always be able to afford that. But here I am up in the clouds. That's incredibly lucky. Through the use of my talent, I've always been able to come up with the rent. Sometimes I feel that that's my main success.

JOANN M. HUNTER: When I came to New York on a three-month scholarship I lived with my dance teacher's friend's sister—a woman I didn't know. It was so uncomfortable because I had to share her bed! At nighttime I would lie still as a board because I didn't want to disturb her and when I sleep I'm usually a sprawler. It was so weird. The next time I came to the city I found an all-woman's hotel and it was clean enough, but what I didn't know was most of the people who were released from Bellevue lived there. I had one tiny room and used the communal bathroom down the hall. I lived there for about three months, dealing with the crazies in the elevator, then I found a cheaper hotel room with my own shower that was closer to the dance studios. I was so proud of myself for finding such a better deal. When I told Chuck Kelly where I was living he said, "Where?!" Little did I know that my new hotel was right off Times Square back when that area was seedy. But I was young, only looking at what appealed to me in the city, and oblivious to the bad part. I never noticed the hookers and they never bothered me.

As soon as you arrive, connect yourself with one studio while you check out others. The large studios like Broadway Dance Center and STEPS are magnets for dancers. You will meet other newcomers, overhear audition and housing information, and have access to their bulletin boards, which list everything from apartment sublets to massage therapy to "Free cat to good home." When you find work, ask your theatrical coworkers if they know of a place. It could happen that a classmate or coworker has a roommate who is going out of town and you can fill their slot.

Sublets are terrific. The furniture, kitchenware, bathroom towels, TV, and tape deck are usually already there. Finding one is a matter of asking friends, searching callboards, and keeping your ears open to pending tours. If you are a member of Equity, check their callboard for sublets. If you have a friend in Equity, ask if they'll check for you. Whether you end up being a roommate or you take a sublet, please be responsible. The property is not yours. This does not give you license to abuse the property, but rather to take better care of it than if it were your own. Talk with ten people who have sublet their apartments and you will hear ten horror stories.

LUIS PEREZ: I sublet my apartment to a family whose daughter was on a ballet scholarship, and when I returned, the place was destroyed—dirty, TV broken, stereo wacked out, and an old sandwich stuck in the VCR. I don't know—maybe her little brother thought it was a toaster. I couldn't believe the parents would be such pigs.

Sometimes it is the person who is subletting from the leaseholder who gets the raw end of the deal. I was in a guy's apartment for about six months, paying the utilities and mailing the rent check to him. During the latter part of my stay, I learned that he was charging me twice the rent and pocketing the rest. Sure, it was his prerogative and my stupidity, but as a struggling dancer it really angered me.

Many times the sublet won't be legal. In these cases your mail will have to come in care of the lessee, all bills will have to be paid by the person, and if asked, you are a family member or friend who is just visiting. Be punctual with sending your payments to the lessee since it is his responsibility to get the rent in on time. If you can get a legal sublet, all the better. You are guaranteed a proper rent and you have the same rights as the original lessee.

Once you have the finances, you will want to get your own apartment. In Manhattan, the rates range upwards from $1200/month for a studio, $1600 for a one-bedroom, and over $2,000 for two or more bedrooms. Be ready to downscale; New York apartments have a definition all their own. What is called a studio may be a windowless large closet, the bathtub may be in the kitchen in a one-bedroom, and a two-bedroom could be a one-bedroom cut in half.

To afford the rent, most young people have roommates. Your monthly nut for rent, utilities, phone, and so forth is cut in as many ways as people sharing the apartment. Often only one person's name goes onto the lease (the one with the most credit), so be very careful to hash out your rights ahead of time. Check the lease and see how many people are allowed in the apartment. The superintendent will see you coming and going and your name will be on the mailbox. You don't want to get kicked out.

With the high costs, many people look for apartments uptown in Harlem and Washington Heights, in the surrounding boroughs of Queens, Brooklyn, and the Bronx, or across the river into New Jersey. The commute may be longer by subway, PATH train, or bus, but the lower rents are a plus. Also, the subway costs the same no matter if you go two stops or twenty. The biggest disadvantages are not being able to dash home if you have a couple of hours to kill and having less frequent trains if you decide to party in the city late at night.

LUIS PEREZ: My mother's friend lived in the Village so I stayed with her family for about a month. Then I shared a little studio, an illegal sublet, with two female dancers from Florida. After that another friend and I got an apartment in Queens that became a revolving door of temporary roommates. Finally I got my own apartment in the Village.

Once you get an apartment, use your imagination to furnish it cheaply. You need a bed, yes, but not a full bedroom suite. A mattress on the floor is fine. If you can afford a futon or a pull-out sofa, you kill two birds with one stone. Need a bookshelf? Use bricks and a piece of plywood. Old milk crates are great as end tables and for storage. Curtains are expensive so buy colorful sheets, hem the top, and stick a curtain rod through them. They may seem dull from the outside, but you have privacy. Think function, not Laura Ashley.

Secondhand stores and the Salvation Army have old bureaus for clothes, and many space-saving stores dedicate their lines to storage products. If you can carry the items home, enlisting some help from friends, you'll save on delivery charges. Household furniture and items can also be found at apartment and neighborhood tag sales so check out fliers and small newspapers.

The streets of New York are a wonderland of thrown-out goodies. Don't be embarrassed to scrounge. No one drives to the dump to get rid of old possessions—it's all out on the street, prime for the picking before the trash collectors come. However, I would stay away from anything stuffed, like a mattress or sofa. All the disinfectant spray in the world may not be able to challenge bugs, questionable stains, and mysterious odors.

No one expects the Taj Mahal from a struggling artist. As long as you never limit your perspective, thinking that an item is useable only as the manufacturer intends, you can furnish your apartment with little money and a lot of fun.

Your first housing experiences may be nightmares. The apartment building may be a dump, or your roommate may be the type who only leaves a quarter inch of milk in the carton, but hang in tight. The more theatrical work you get, the more your living situation will improve. Create a busy schedule for yourself: classes, auditions, support jobs, libraries, street fairs, and walking through different sections of the city. You will enrich yourself and keep away the blues.

Dance Classes

The best way to get free or greatly reduced dance classes is to go on scholarship. Since studios are privately owned, scholarships are not the same as the ones you apply for in college. Your SAT scores mean nothing. Instead, the scholarship is based on your desire to learn, your dependability, your level of training, and your financial situation. In return for the free classes you will be assigned various duties that help in the maintenance of the studio.

Each individual studio has its own criteria and process of application. For some programs, you must audition or send a videotape. Some expect a certain level of training, like at STEPS and Broadway Dance Center, and at others you can be a beginner, like at New Dance Group. Registration fees vary. The common denominators in the work-study programs are that you must agree to devote two to six months of your time and to be available to work for ten to twelve hours a week in exchange for classes. To find scholarship information for each studio, visit their websites, call them, or simply stop by and ask.

The work requirement varies from studio to studio. Usual jobs are signing people in; collecting money; some computer work if you have the skills; cleaning bathrooms, dressing rooms, studios, mirrors; working the boutique or café; helping with mailings; and serving food and beverages at galas or performances. If you cannot be there one day, you may be responsible for switching hours with another scholarship student. The jobs will be assigned to you as need be. As in any situation, some people will be lazier than others. Don't gripe. Remember that the studio is doing you a huge favor, and your cooperation will be remembered and appreciated.

If you fail to get a scholarship at one studio, seek out another. Sometimes smaller studios have more opportunities. On the other hand, larger studios may have more turnover. Try not to set your heart on one studio. As long as the classes are good, you can spend three months at one studio while you plan to audition for another.

If you are not on scholarship, you can cut your costs by buying dance cards instead of single classes. Usually the cards are for ten classes, to be used in a specified number of weeks. The discount is usually about 10 percent off—ten classes for the price of nine or eleven for the price of ten. Certain schools connected with dance companies require the purchase of a dance card. It makes sense. You are studying a particular technique and one class is not enough to get the hang of it.

If you choose a particular studio because their prices are lower, use your common sense. Will you have to take the subway to get there, automatically increasing your round trip by four dollars? Are the teachers appropriate for your level? On the other hand, are you going to a more expensive studio because it's the "in" place to be? Often smaller studios will give you more personal attention and have fine teachers who devote themselves to the development of the student.

No matter where you take class, you want to get the most out of it. If possible, rather than run into the class completely cold, warm up well ahead of time. Every dancer knows the fundamentals of a particular style that they can do alone. Give yourself a mini barre, stretch well, or work on contractions and isolations. You will get a double benefit in class. Instead of using the barre or warm-up to get the kinks out, you will work toward perfecting the technique. It is undeniable how good you feel in a second class because the first limbered your body. Imagine if you help yourself to feel that way in the first class. You don't need a studio to work by yourself. Any small space in your apartment where you can extend one arm to the side is large enough. Warming up in the studio is great, but many times it turns into a gabfest. Concentrate on yourself ahead of time and you will be amazed at the improvement in class.

A second self-help method is to watch and imitate. Many studios have glass walls or doors where you can observe an ongoing class. Choose a particular movement and when you get home, try to do it. (Doing it in the hallway may not be appreciated.) Bit by bit you will pick up the style. Look at professional dance photos from your own book collection, in the library, or from magazines. Study the lines of the bodies and imitate them. Check yourself in a mirror or ask your roommate what the difference is between you and the photo. It may seem goofy, but you are absorbing one more move for free.

JIM BORSTELMANN: When I got into Harkness House on scholarship, I loved it. How could you not? The marble staircases, the chandeliers, Rebecca Harkness' ashes in "The Chalice of Life" created by Salvador Dalí, the bejeweled elevator that took you to class . . . I took company class, then men's class, then partnering. Lee Theodore taught jazz downstairs so I'd sneak down and watch through the door and think, "This is where I want to be." Later I was on scholarship at STEPS for a full year but I never took class. I just liked being there, signing everyone in, and watching the classes. I got so much out of watching people do it. I never get how people can't just look and imitate the style. You can't teach that "thing." You just do it.

A third self-help method is almost laughably obvious.

<u>MAMIE DUNCAN-GIBBS:</u> As I started auditioning more, I realized that I was getting free dance classes. Sometimes I didn't even want the job; I just wanted to work on my music.

Voice and Acting Classes

Since dance is your primary target, it is unlikely you can go on scholarship for voice or acting. These positions are for the singers and actors who focus on each particular craft. However, there are ways to cut costs.

Many teachers conduct classes from their homes. Once you have taken a few classes and if you feel comfortable, ask if you can clean their apartment, run errands, or help with business mail in exchange for instruction. It may not be fun, but four hours of cleaning is about the same price as a class. You save money and the teacher doesn't have to pay for a service.

Although studying voice every week is prime, you can cut it down to twice a month or less. Be sure to tape record your vocal exercises during your lessons and be diligent about practicing on your own. The vocal muscles will develop, though without benefit of correction. Consistently go over your audition songs, and if an important audition is coming up, spend the money to go back to your teacher for guidance.

Just as in voice, you must pay for your acting classes. Compare class sizes, frequency, and payment scales. Since you will not be entering a full-time program, you need the classes to fit into your schedule. Make sure you have enough time to prepare for each class so you get its full benefit. Observing other actors is interesting, but ultimately you must perform monologues or scenes in class for critique.

To save money on scripts and vocal scores, make the Library of Performing Arts your second home. They carry a staggering amount of sheet music, audio scores, and plays. Many are in the circulating library so you can take them home, but some you must peruse only on the premises. However, copy machines are available at a small cost. Many of the plays are in the Humanities division on Fifth Avenue at 42nd Street. If you have access to the Internet, you can find the location of what you need at www.nypl.org. Otherwise the staff is extremely helpful. The beauty is that all of this vast information is free.

MAMIE DUNCAN-GIBBS: Survival without money—that's me. I was broke so I had to learn to sing on my own. I lived at the Lincoln Center Library for the Performing Arts. At the time I couldn't really sight read but I would choose Broadway show tunes, get the record—they didn't have CDs back then—get the vocal score, and sing along with it. I looked how the notes went up and down and basically learned to sight read like that. I just kept praying and saying, "Okay, I'm going to do this. I have to do this. I don't have to be rich to do this. I can figure this out."

Dance Wear

The cost of dance shoes can't be avoided, unless you happen to find your size in the lost and found or in the discount box at a dancewear shop. Maintenance is the key to making your shoes last a long time. Apply dance rubber to the soles and replace it as soon as it wears out or tears. Brace heels and have straps resewn as soon as they begin to shred. (A good cobbler can double the leather at the stress point.) Although it isn't pretty, wrap gaffers tape around tears and splits in ballet or flat shoes; they are fine for class. Once you have broken in various shoes, keep your favorites aside for auditions.

It is not wise to be cheap when it comes to buying shoes. Your feet are an essential tool of your career. A bad fit over time can cause injuries, bone spurs, corns, and inflamed bunions. If the cheap shoes feel comfortable, great. But don't scrimp if you feel like plunging your feet in a bucket of ice ten minutes after you put them on. If the standard sizes don't mold to your foot, investigate custom-made shoes. They cost quite a bit, but they will last for years since the leather is of high quality and your feet won't be fighting the fit.

Some productions allow you to keep your shoes at the end of the run or as the shoes get too raggedy. Ask the wardrobe head what the policy is or offer to buy the shoes at a discount. There is an Equity rule that no dancer can wear another dancer's shoes so you may luck out. Many producers sell the old shoes to costume houses, but it is worth a try.

As far as dance clothes, avoid the lure of fashion. Although it is fun to have designer T-shirts, they won't make your arabesque any higher. You can survive with two sets of clothing, plus an audition outfit, until you can afford more for variety. In Chapter 7 I give you tips for choosing the right outfits for both class and auditions.

Hesitate before throwing out regular street clothes. If a sweatshirt shrinks, can you cut off the sleeves and V the neck? If a button-down shirt is buttonless, can you tie it at the waist over a leotard? Can floodwater-length sweatpants be turned into hip warmers? Can old holey socks be made into foot and ankle warmers, and T-shirts with armpit stains cut into sleeveless tanks? The possibilities are as endless as your wardrobe.

Always check the discount box at the dance store for deals on tights and leotards. Also, the lost and found box at a dance studio can be a treasure trove as long as the item is nondescript and has been there for a while. How mortifying it would be to hear, "Hey you, that's my shirt!" as you enter class. If you do pick something from the lost and found, never, never wear it without laundering it first. A friendly cockroach, louse, spider, or crab might consider it—or you—a new home.

Just as with shoes, maintenance again comes into vital play for your clothes. If you don't know how to sew a basic stitch, learn. Holes and runs can be mended before they turn gargantuan or humiliating, especially in the crotch area. Hand washing your clothes in the sink saves a great deal of money. As long as you scrub the armpits and crotches well and rinse thoroughly, your dancewear will be clean and will hold up for a long time. Since dance clothes are made to resist moisture, they normally dry overnight draped over your shower rod. They may feel a little stiff, but that will pass as soon as you put them on.

If you use a washing machine, avoid overly hot water and dryers for stretchy clothes; the elastic will soon crackle. Lingerie bags are excellent to keep the stretchy clothes from winding their way to oblivion during the spin cycle. Although it smells sweet and feels comfy, don't go overboard on fabric softener, nor soak your clothes too long in products like Woolite. I am not a scientist, but a renowned wardrobe head advised me that too much can break down the fabric.

Transportation

In a word, walk. Figure a minute per block, two to three minutes per avenue, and walk whenever and wherever you can. You won't be alone. No one except the wealthy consistently drive within the city. Commuters drive in and out, people get away for the weekend, but the traffic and parking within Manhattan on a daily basis are cost prohibitive, maddening, and just plain hell.

When you can't walk, use the subway and bus systems. As of May 1, 2003, a single fare is $2.00, but you can save money by buying a Metro-Card. An Unlimited Use card for seven days costs $21, and for thirty days $70. This type is extremely helpful if you have to bop all around town going to classes, work, auditions, and so on. Pay-Per-Ride offers six rides for the price of five, and a Fun Pass allows unlimited use for one day for only $7. This is a real bargain if you know that one day is going to be particularly hectic.

The MetroCard can be used for all subways and buses. You can transfer for free from bus to subway, subway to bus, or bus to bus within a two-hour period. This feature is helpful if you have quick errands to run on the East Side where there are fewer subway lines. For updated prices, rules, and restrictions, contact the NYC Transit by phone or on the Web.

Taxis hustle through the city, but the fares can add up quickly if you are stuck in traffic. Be aware of nonavailability in the morning and evening rush hours, around 4:30 P.M. when many go off duty, before matinees on Wednesdays, and between 7:30 P.M. and 8 P.M. when people are rushing to the theatre. Riding solo is obviously more expensive than with two or three others. As a matter of fact, on a short ride you will save money if you travel with three other people rather than take the subway. But the wisest choice is to save taking taxis unless you are in an extreme hurry or for late-night hours when the subways and walking are more dangerous on quiet streets.

Pictures and Resumes

These are such important components of auditions, I have devoted a chapter to discussing not only their costs, but also how to secure good ones that represent you and your experience. Please refer to Chapter 8.

Laundry

As I mentioned earlier, hand washing your dance clothes saves money. However, hand washing your entire wardrobe is a bit unrealistic. You will need to spend money to use a washing machine. In every neighborhood there are scores of Laundromats, and some buildings have their own coin-operated laundry room. Most Laundromats offer drop-off service. Although it is convenient, you will pay extra for this service.

There are three ways to cut costs. First, bring your own laundry detergent and fabric softener. Those little machines with the cute packets of detergent are good in a pinch but they will mount your costs. Second, wash your laundry when you have a full load. The washing machine won't give you a cut rate for a half load. Third, buy clothes that are machine washable to avoid monstrous dry-cleaning bills.

Having an apartment-size washer and dryer is great, but many landlords do not allow them. Since they pay the water and fuel bills, you are increasing their expenses by using these conveniences. If you want to sneak one in, remember that the landlord can monitor how much water each apartment uses, the superintendent can enter your apartment for repairs and may discover your secret, and if the machine floods, you've got more than a floor-full of hot water on your hands.

Hair, Makeup, Toiletries

When you walk the streets of Manhattan you will be amazed at the large proportion of good-looking people. The city is a beehive of performers, models, and artists, as well as top-notch business people. The competition is fierce and looking good is a necessity. There is also an extreme amount of wealth. Such an atmosphere breeds high costs for personal care services. However, you don't need to break your bank to look your best.

The rage of low-cost, walk-in hair salons that has swept the country also exists in New York. For under $20 you can get a decent haircut.

Knowing exactly what you want is important to ensure a good cut, rather than saying, "Just do what you want." In some establishments the hairdressers are trained in only certain styles, so if you can't point to a picture in their book with full knowledge that your hair type can withstand the cut, avoid them.

Whatever show you work on, in or out of New York, make friends with the hairdressers. Many are more than willing to give you a haircut in their spare time either at home or in the theatre for a reduced rate. You may get caught up on theatre gossip at the same time.

Hair coloring, highlights, body waves, and straightening are at your discretion. If you can do it yourself, all the better. If not, compare prices at various salons in different neighborhoods. Hair weaves in Harlem are much cheaper than on Fifth Avenue, the West Side tends to be less than the East Side, and salons downtown near the East Village are less if you avoid the chi-chi streets.

Unless your skin is problematic, shop for makeup and toiletries for everyday use at discount stores. Compare sales and specials at different stores, and if it's a brand you like, buy a few instead of just one. Something as simple as using a cheaper deodorant bath soap can save you a few dollars. Most stores accept coupons so check the fliers in the Sunday papers. As long as you stick to the essentials for a look that is good for you and avoid the temptation to try every latest fashion color, you will cut costs.

Until you have the extra money and unless you are auditioning for film and television, manicures and pedicures are luxuries you can forego. No casting person will hire a dancer because they have great fingernails and your toes will be hidden in your shoes. As a matter of fact, long nails can be dangerous to other dancers around you or to your dance partner. Bold colors also stop the line of your arm. However, if you feel naked without polish, put it on only for auditions.

Theatre Admission

For the price of one orchestra seat for a Broadway show, you can get a Head Shot Special, pay a quarter of your rent, take ten dance classes, or feed yourself for two weeks; all of these options passed up for one two-and-a-half-hour period in a theatre. Yet viewing theatre is essential to all dancers. How can you afford it? There are several ways.

The Theatre Development Fund (TDF) is an organization that promotes theatre by offering discount tickets to Broadway, Off-Broadway, and a variety of music and dance performances. They have booths, called TKTS, located in Times Square and in lower Manhattan at South Street Seaport. You can buy tickets at half- to three-quarters price (plus a $3 per ticket service charge) on the day of the performance by merely standing in line. The posted shows change daily and throughout the day, depending on availability. Be ready to pay with cash or travelers' checks.

If you qualify, you can be on the TDF mailing list at a minimal yearly cost. Every four to six weeks you receive at least three offers to specific performances of shows and dance companies at a great discount. Broadway tickets go for about $25. The seats may not be the best, but the deals are terrific. To qualify you must be a student, a teacher, a union member, a retired person, a performing arts professional, a member of the clergy, or a member of the armed forces. If you are not a student of a high school or college, ask the director of the dance studio where you normally take class to state that you are a student. If someone in your family qualifies, ask them to sign up. The tickets come in the mail and no one questions the identity of the person who occupies the theatre seat.

TDF also offers vouchers for over three hundred Off-Off Broadway theatres and production companies. For $28, you receive four open admissions, good for a year from the date of purchase. The theatres range from tiny lofts to well-established theatres like The Joyce. Visit the Theatre Development Fund website at www.tdf.org to download an application or to find out more information.

Other traditional sources for discount tickets can be found online by searching through www.allthatchat.com for discount codes, or by becoming a free member of Playbill Online. Taking out a subscription to theatres like the Public, Manhattan Theater Club, and Lincoln Center will give you tickets at a lower price, especially if you sign up for previews. Most Broadway theatres offer "rush" seats (seats in the first two or three rows) and standing room on the day of the performance. Ask at each box office to find out their policies. On the whole, as nice as it is to have orchestra seats, opt for the cheaper balcony seats, and attend matinees when the prices are lower. Ask if the box office offers student discounts.

Look in restaurants and stores for "twofers." The coupon looks like a regular theatre ticket, and although you may not actually get two for the price of one, you will get a discount.

Both the New York Shakespeare Festival in Central Park and Lincoln Center, among other establishments, offer free performances during the summer. Check the newspapers or call each foundation to get details. It may mean a wait in line, but it is worth the effort.

Now for some of the less traditional ways to see theatre.

<u>LUIS PEREZ:</u> When I was in the Joffrey, a group of us would hang outside Lincoln Center every night to second or third act the ballets. Invariably some bored businessman would leave after the first act, dragging his wife behind him. We'd tell them we were dance students and ask for their ticket stubs. Sometimes we'd stand under the outdoor balcony at New York State Theater during intermission and ask people to throw down their stubs. Then we'd go in, wait until everyone sat down, and would find empty seats in the balcony. I didn't ever not get in for at least one of the acts.

Second acting Broadway shows can be a little trickier. You will have no problem walking in during intermission, but a surly usher may question you when you choose an empty seat. Head for the balcony and look for a group of empty seats as opposed to one or two. Remember that some people get stuck in long bathroom lines and don't make it back to their seats before the second act begins. Stay away from hit shows where tickets are at a premium. Weekly box office grosses listed in the newspapers or online will give you a good idea which shows are not selling as well as others.

Many shows hand out free tickets ("paper" the house) when they want to ensure a good audience. These listings are posted at Equity, usually on the day of the performance, and are also offered to staff members of production companies. In theatres, sign-up sheets are often posted ahead of time for cast members. If you are friendly with someone in a show, ask them to sign up for you if they don't want to use the tickets themselves.

Every new show has an open dress rehearsal before the first preview. Everyone associated with the show—creators, cast, crew, producers, publicity, and so on—is allowed to invite a certain number of people.

Ask around and keep your ears open for possible invitations. Do you take class with someone in the show? Do you know anyone in stage management? Does a friend work for the producers or agents of one of the actors? Sometimes tickets are issued and sometimes there is an invitation list. As a last resort, you could show up at the theatre and see if people are simply entering. You may be able to con your way in.

Some dancers have become ushers for theatres or work the concession stands in the lobby. The positive side is that you get to see shows for free. The negative is that you see the same show over and over and the work is a long-term commitment. Many Off-Broadway or nonprofit theatres welcome volunteers to usher, man the concession stand, or do various other duties. In return you get to see the show for free. This volunteer work is on a short-term basis so it's a pretty good deal.

Although seeing live theatre is the optimum, viewing productions on video or television is second best. The Lincoln Center Library for the Performing Arts has a vast collection of shows and dance concerts that can be viewed in house. Some shows require permission from the creators before they can be seen, but others are open. The PBS television stations often air theatrical productions or dance specials. Keep your eye on the television guide and tune in when you can. The best part is, it's free.

Food

If you curb your taste buds and your indulgences, you will save so much money. Do you really need a super cappuccino and gourmet muffin at a coffee bar for breakfast, or can you brew your own coffee, scramble a couple of eggs, or dive into a bowl of cereal at home? Are you able to fill a cup of ramen noodles with boiling water or do you need to be served at a Japanese restaurant? Is it really necessary to order a roast beef, Muenster, and tomato sandwich at the deli, or will egg salad or peanut butter and jelly suffice? You don't need to turn into a health freak or bore your palate to save money, but you must be wise about your choices and not be too lazy.

We are in an age of convenience food—fast, fully prepared, microwaveable. However, you pay extra for the convenience and often don't get as much nutrition as if you prepared the same meal yourself. Take a look at a Big Mac. You can buy a full pound of better-grade hamburger for the cost of the sandwich. Add in the price of a Coke and french fries, and you can buy not only the pound of hamburger, but also a head of lettuce, two tomatoes, a quarter pound of cheese, and a loaf of bread. That's enough for several meals. Trade the Super Meal for vegetables, and you have enough food for a week of dinners.

Although variety is the spice of life, you'll save more money by spreading the same ingredients over time. For example, a stew loaded with vegetables or a batch of spaghetti sauce with meat is filling and can last for days. Buy a pound of lunchmeat or make a tuna salad with tons of celery, and you have daily sandwiches to pack with you. Rice and pasta taste good with any meat or vegetable, or are filling all alone. Fruit is terrific, as long as you stick with the cheaper apples or bananas and skip the four-dollar raspberries in the dead of winter.

LUIS PEREZ: To budget, I ate a lot of rice and beans. Some nights it would be just a head of lettuce or broccoli thrown on spaghetti. A lot of eggplant for a while because it was thirty-nine cents a pound. Now I can't look at it. I'd eat anything that was really cheap. A Russian dancer taught me the trick of the heating coil to save money on tour. You plug up the sink in the hotel, boil the water with a half dozen eggs, and you've got dinner plus breakfast the next day. Another trick is to bring Tupperware or a Ziploc bag to a restaurant that has an all-you-can-eat salad bar. Get a plate of salad, pour it into the container in your dancebag, then go back for another plate. Of course, that's illegal but . . .

When buying food, really check out prices. Grocery stores and delis that are literally next door to each other can sell the same product for a difference of dollars. Bargains can be found at large stores like Fairway (just below STEPS dance studio); at the meat, fish, and vegetable markets on Ninth Avenue in the low 40's; at small, unfancy local delis, and at food stores in Chinatown. Scope out your neighborhood, and if prices are too high, consider buying food near where you work or take class. Buy whatever is on sale that week and in bulk when you can. For example, a six-pack of Snickers will be less in the long run than picking one up on six separate occasions at a candy store. If you have a halfway decent refrigerator, which unfortunately is not usually the case, buy meats on sale and freeze them. Stay away from name brands for condiments, tomato sauce, cereals, and the like, and stick to in-store brands. In many cases all you are paying for is fancy packaging with the name brands.

MICHAEL KUBALA: When I first went to NYU, the girls were eating baby food because it was cheap, nutritious, and easily digestible. I started eating tapioca and strained carrots, yogurt and apples. It was okay. Now at least there's a lot more fruit and vegetables to choose from.

Whenever you can, carry food and drinks with you to avoid the temptation of buying something when your stomach gurgles. If you are caught in the middle of a hunger pang, choose the cheaper delis or head for the reliable standby, a pizza place. Street vendors who sell hotdogs, bagels, or fruit are super cheap. Buying a twenty-cent banana from a vendor is far better than a fruit salad from a salad bar at $3.99 a pound. Carry an empty water bottle with you. All dance studios and larger hotels have water fountains or water coolers where you can fill up. Save your empty Gatorade or Snapple bottles to refill at home with juice or tea. If you can't stand the tepid temperature, invest in a cheap insulated drink carrier to keep the drink cool.

If your part-time job is in a restaurant, you've got an advantage. Most restaurants let you eat one meal, either before or after your shift. Some give you a break for a snack if your hours are long. You may have to eat whatever is offered for that day, but at least it's food. While you are working, you may be allowed to drink an appropriate amount of soda. As hateful and tiring as waiting tables can be, the benefit of free food outweighs working in an office where you don't even get paid for the lunch hour. If you do work in a nonfood business, brown bag your lunch and eat either in the employees' lounge or outside in a park.

Once you are working in a theatrical job, keep up with your budgeting. Admittedly, it's a great feeling to go out with cast members for lunch to trade histories and gossip. But if you brown bag it, you save money and are granted an hour to an hour and a half of free time. No rehearsal studio closes down during lunch. It is a quiet time to regather energy. The choreographer and stage manager often eat in to get caught up on work, discuss schedules, or simply to rest. You can study, read, review steps, chat, run chores, or nap to ward off the late-afternoon slump during rehearsals. In some shows the choreographic demands are less so you can do a barre or work out to keep yourself in top form.

Although you might be alone the first few days, you will find that by your example more people will follow suit.

When I was new to Broadway lunchtime was an agony for me. Eating too much in the middle of the day upset my stomach and made me sleepy, I was trying to save money, and I was incredibly shy about inviting myself to join the seasoned professionals at a restaurant. So I would eat something small like a yogurt, do a barre, and being a crossword fanatic, I'd immerse myself in a puzzle. What I didn't realize was that these actions were noticed by the cast and choreographer alike. Although they would kid me, my reputation grew for being incredibly self-motivated, self-reliant, and a credit to my profession. They never guessed that I was really a poor, shy dancer who happened to love doing barre.

Miscellaneous Tips

Can't afford to buy newspapers every day? Go to Grand Central Station to the Metro North train platforms. There are open recyclable bins in the track areas where commuters deposit their papers. Don't feel like an idiot hunting for the sections you want. Many people do it. You may not get to do the crossword, but the papers are relatively clean.

Banking can be a problem if you don't have enough deposited to avoid monthly service charges. Check out savings banks if you don't need to write checks, and compare percentage rates and withdrawal policies. If you already have a bank account at a national bank at home, investigate if there are any branches in New York City. You may be able to simply change your mailing address and not have to open a new account. One way to avoid service charges is to keep a CD in the bank for the combined accounts total that provides free checking. If you don't have the money yourself, ask your parents. You never spend the money and it would accumulate interest for them. The CD would have to be in your name, so you would have to promise to renew the CD at maturity and not pocket the money yourself. Of course, if you dishonestly dip into the funds, you ruin your balance and your eligibility to get free checking, and your parents might disown you.

Postage stamps can add up when paying bills. Rather than using the mail, you can pay at the specific company, if it is within walking distance from your home or work. (Spending money on the subway rather defeats the purpose.) At most check-cashing services you can pay your telephone bill for free. However, there may be a fee for other utility or cable bills up to a dollar, so in that case, the postage stamp is a better deal. These establishments usually offer food stamps, lottery tickets, or accept bets for OTB (off-track betting), so you may have to wait in line. Just don't be tempted to blow your money on a hot tip for June Belle to come in first in the sixth race at Belmont.

If you have credit cards, try not to use them. This "magic money" gives you an unrealistic view of your finances at this point in your career. When you are struggling, the old-fashioned way is best. Allow yourself to carry only a certain amount of cash each day. You won't be able to exceed the limit because you simply don't have it. Debit cards are fine because the money is automatically deducted from your bank account. But keep a watchful eye on your account to be sure you have enough at the end of the month to pay bills. The fact is, plastic is not real and too many people have gotten into financial debt because of it.

You absolutely need an answering machine or service to receive calls about prospective jobs. However, do you really need a cell phone or beeper? Unless you have an agent who needs to contact you on the spur of the moment for auditions, cell phones and beepers are unnecessary expenses. Consider: Are most of your conversations work related or do they lean toward where you plan to meet your friends, what groceries need to be picked up, or what's new in gossip? Will a twenty-five cent public phone call do the trick?

The heat in the city during the summer can be unbearable. If you want an air conditioner, check out small repair shops that rebuild appliances before you opt for a spanking new one. Once you get one, don't run it unless the weather is sizzling so that your electric bill won't skyrocket. Unfortunately, a window air conditioner blocks any breezes, so remember on balmy days to use just the fan option. If you don't like air-conditioning, consider installing a rotating ceiling fan.

Remember that you pay for whatever is turned on in your apartment, except for the water tap and heat. Cooking a roast for three hours will cost you more in gas or electricity than broiling for ten minutes. Instead of vegetating on the sofa watching too much TV, veg out with a good book borrowed from the library. Turn off lights, use battery-operated clocks, and unplug any electronic device that is not in constant use. You may feel like a pioneer or a product of the Depression, but you will save money penny by penny.

If your budget is really tight, be creative with reusable items. A plastic bread bag comes with its own twisty-tie and, when washed, is as good as a Baggie. Any plastic grocery bag or wrap can cover leftover food. Margarine, ice cream, and soup buckets are the poor man's Tupperware. Save extra sugar and sweetener packs when you buy a cup of coffee. (Once when doing a low-budget workshop we saved so many sugar packs I was able to bake a cake!) Wash out any glass jar—food, makeup, but not anything containing poisonous substances—to use as storage containers for small items. Egg cartons are great for storing earrings, safety pins, or hardware. Clothes pins and a cardboard box can organize your mail. The list is endless if you examine every item for other possibilities before automatically throwing it away.

As an animal lover, I know that pets can be best friends, especially when you are new to a huge city like New York. However, Tabby or Toto may not be worth the cost of their coziness at this point in your life. Besides the high cost of food, litter, vaccinations, and mysterious illnesses or injuries, boarding your pet when you go out of town on a job, which may happen frequently, is terribly expensive. A new roommate in your future may have allergies. The perfect apartment you find at a low cost may not allow animals. If your day extends over many hours of taking class, auditioning, and carrying a support job, who is going to walk the pooch? Once you become established in your career, sure, go ahead and offer a great home to the animal of your choice. In the meantime, if you need an animal fix, watch the dogs play in the various dedicated runs throughout the city, volunteer at an animal shelter, or make some extra money animal-sitting for friends or by working for a dog-walking service and in the many animal daycare centers that are cropping up in various neighborhoods.

Moving to New York City does not have to be an impossible financial feat if you plan and live wisely. No matter how inflation or terrible disasters alter prices, where there is a will, there is a way to survive. I guarantee you that within each dance studio, many students will be in the same boat as you, struggling for the job that will give you some security. Rest assured that the struggle itself is an exciting ride that builds fortitude, patience, and powerful memories.

CHAPTER SEVEN

Wear and When: Dance Clothes for Class and Auditions

I really am from the school of Shut Up and Dance. If I were to teach I would be a disciplinarian. When I did Bring Back Birdie *all the kids arrived with their sweaters wrapped around their hips—their outfits. I would ask why they had their hips covered like that. Nothing is better than all black or all pink because then you see the muscle. Dance clothing is for a purpose; it is not an excuse to not dance well.*

— Chita Rivera

In the same way that a normal person wouldn't wear jeans and a T-shirt to a job interview, there is a distinct difference between what you wear to dance class as opposed to an audition. While you can wear most audition clothes to a class, the "dressing down" that you can get away with in class can look messy in an audition. Likewise, what may be perfectly suitable for a ballet or modern class would look completely wrong for musical theatre. Knowing what to wear in different situations helps to present yourself to your best advantage.

What to Wear in a Professional Class

Each style of dance has its own dress code mostly for practicality and partially from a fashion standpoint. Before you dress for class, think:

Will this aggravate me, cause me possible injury, inhibit me, or make the teacher dial 911 for the fashion police? You want to feel comfortable and look like a professional. Presenting the right image shows that you are serious and savvy. Many choreographers observe dance classes for prospects, and likewise, many choreographers teach class themselves.

JULIO MONGE: Maurice Hines was choreographing *Satchmo* and he saw me in class and said, "I want you to come to my audition for my new show." He wanted me, so I got in. That was my first Equity job.

You don't need the lashes and the hair gel—as a matter of fact, if you come in too coiffed, you'll look weird. (Only performers who are taking classes between shows can get away with that.) Do wear deodorant and avoid dousing yourself in heavy colognes or musky oils. There is nothing worse when you are huffing and puffing than inhaling a mouthful of someone's stale odor. Be neat, be ready to sweat, and be assured that dressing properly will make you feel more at home in a strange studio.

Some schools have a dress code. Simply ask and they will be happy to tell you. In New York City, there will be a dress code only in certain ballet or modern schools, not studios. The general rules for studios are these:

Tap Class Clothing

Women, wear tights and leotards, jazz pants and a T-shirt or button-down shirt tied at the waist, or street clothes if they don't inhibit your movement. Skirts on the whole are unwise for women and long skirts are taboo. A caught heel in the hem makes for a nasty fall. Men, it may be a New York thing, but you tend to look dorky in tights and leotards in tap class. Wear jazz pants or street clothes.

Tap Class Shoes

Flat character for men, heels for women, obviously with taps screwed on. Check if your local dancewear store provides the service or recommends a cobbler.

Jazz Class Clothing

Wear tights and leotards, jazz pants and T-shirts, not-too-baggy sweatpants, aerobic-type midriffs and bottoms, or for men, regular pants that you absolutely know you can dance in. As in tap, you may look dorky in tights and leotards. (There's just something about the way an oxford-type shoe looks on the ankle—rather Ichabod Crane-ish.) Be careful of too much exposed skin on your legs or back so that you don't get floor burns if you do any slides. If you haven't purchased pre-cut tights, cut the feet of your tights either across the ball of the foot or lengthwise along the instep, whichever you prefer, because many jazz teachers do warm-up in bare feet. Aerobic wear is intended to emphasize muscle mass, whereas dancewear sleekens, so be forewarned that you may look stubby in that type of clothing. Women, you will never go wrong if you stick with leotards and tights. Ballet tights in a jazz class can be a little unhip, but, on the other hand, it may look like you are so diligent you ran right from ballet class to jazz. Throw a T-shirt and some leg warmers in your dancebag if you want to dress down or keep warm.

Jazz Class Shoes

Both men and women will need flat jazz shoes or boots, with or without the soles split, split-soled jazz sneakers, and heels for women. Before you run out and buy all the styles, see what the students tend to use in class or the teacher prefers. Women, I beg you: I know it feels great to dance in jazz sneakers but remember that in most shows you will be wearing heels. High heels. I have seen many a supposedly fine dancer look like an amateur when the costume designer pours them into three-or-more-inchers. Some develop knee and back injuries because the muscle training and balance are totally different. Also, too much time in jazz sneakers can make your leg and butt muscles bulky. Heels can become comfortable, even preferable to you, if you give them the necessary time.

LUIS PEREZ: When I had to wear heels in *Phantom of the Opera*, I couldn't understand how girls did it. To this day it astounds me that girls can do the same jetés as we do, the same sauts de basques and everything else, and land on that little platform.

JOANN M. HUNTER: It takes discipline to dance in heels, to do the steps over and over again until you get them right even though your feet hurt so much you can't walk. I never wear flat shoes in rehearsal. If I have to wear them in the show, I wear them in rehearsal so I know what it feels like. That's my mentality.

<u>Bebe Neuwirth</u>: I've danced in ballet shoes, pointe shoes, heels, and barefoot, but for training I'm wary of jazz sneakers. I don't think you can really, really feel your feet—to develop your feet the way you can in ballet slippers or barefoot. It's very important to build up the strength in your feet. People argue that there's a split sole so you can point your feet, but it's more than pointing. There's an articulation and strength that needs to be developed.

Ballet Class Clothing

Wear tights, leotards, or unitards. For women, pink or black tights are preferable with solid basic-colored leotards. The whole point is to create long lines in your body so a lime leotard with scarlet tights is out of the question. Black tights can be worn under a black leotard, but not under any other color. However, black tights can be worn over any color leotard, rolled at the waist, draped over an elastic belt and pulled down over your hips, or pulled up and over the midriff with suspenders. Pink or tan tights look good under any color leotard. Men should wear tights with a leotard or T-shirt, or a unitard. Wear the tights over the leotard, rolled at the waist with an elastic belt, or pulled up with suspenders. Garter fasteners on wide elastic serve as great suspenders. You can undo them and roll the tights at the waist if you feel like a change. The colors for men's tights are usually black or gray. Subtlety is the key. For both sexes, leg warmers are fine, as long as they don't cover your flaws so much you forget about working on them. Half-body or full-body dance woolens are great. They keep you warm and maintain line. T-shirts for women are fine if they are neat. Tie them at the waist or wear an elastic belt to enhance the definition between ribs, waist, and hips. Men, wear a dance belt.

Ballet Class Shoes

Ballet slippers for men and women. Pointe shoes for women if you want and only if you are ready for it. (Yes, you may need pointe. Have you seen *Phantom of the Opera*?) Some advanced dancers wear old pointe shoes with the shanks torn out as ballet slippers. The colors come in pink for women (the usual), and black and white for men. Whatever light-colored shoe you have, if it does not match your leg color, wear a pair of thin white socks to soften the line. For example, black tights with white or pink shoes break the line of your foot, ankle, and calf. Many dancers solve this problem by going barefoot inside their slippers. Tan slippers look great with bare feet.

Not all of the dance wear will be comfortable. Dance clothing enhances line but it also protects your body. For men, the bane is the dance belt.

DAVID WARREN-GIBSON: I saw what you did with a dance belt. You put your legs in and pulled it up. But all the way up? I went, "OH JEEZ! Now what? This is how we live? Like this?!" So I'd pull it down a little bit, I'd like pull it out of my crack and squeeze my butt so it wasn't so uncomfortable.

MICHAEL KUBALA: I felt very odd in tights, exposing my genitalia that way. They were so tight, and that little seam up the back? And the dance belt. The first time I wore one, the teacher said, "Michael, I think you're wearing that wrong. You've got to flip it up." It wasn't my dance belt that was flipped down, it was . . .

LUIS PEREZ: I hadn't practiced how to put a dance belt on at home so for my first class I put it on backwards. I thought the thin end went up the front and the thick end covered your butt. I ended up cutting my balls in half and thinking, "Damn, this hurts. And now we're supposed to move?"

JIM BORSTELMANN: I hated dance belts until I was taught to lift my family jewels. They said, "You're showing the nickel. Don't show the nickel." I thought, "What the hell is he talking about nickel?" I guess it's the head of your weiner. If you don't have it tucked up right, there's this thing that sticks out. As if ballet wasn't complicated enough.

ROBERT MONTANO: For my first jazz class at JoJo's Dance Factory I vividly remember wearing white jazz pants and black leg warmers with white jazz shoes. Man, I thought I was cool! I saw it in *Dance Magazine*. Well, during warm-up I noticed some girls giggling at me. The teacher came over and whispered, "Robert, can I ask you something? Are you wearing a dance belt?" I said, "Are you getting funny with me?" and he says, "Not at all. I'm straight." I said, "No, I'm not wearing one." He says, "Why not?" So I said with defiance, "This is jazz, man, not ballet. I'm wearing jazz pants, man," and he says, "You gotta wear it even with jazz pants. You're showing your tripod!"

JULIO MONGE: Dance belts hurt but I thought that was part of what made you special as a dancer.

Dance shoes can be another bane for both men and women. After a while your shoes will become your friends. As a matter of fact, you will become very picky and protective of these tools. However, at the beginning they may be alien creatures.

MICHAEL KUBALA: The first time I put on tap shoes I thought, "Wow. Slippery."

TOMMY TUNE: At my first recital somebody said to be lucky you need to put money in your shoes so I put nickels and dimes and quarters in my tap shoes. It was really hard to dance. After I did it I knew that it was lucky because I didn't make any mistakes, but it didn't feel good.

CAITLIN CARTER: I got off on heels because I thought they made my legs look thinner and longer. I was one of those weirdos who would do anything in heels. Jump off the building in three-inch spikes? Sure!

DAVID WARREN-GIBSON: Tap shoes: hard, and loud. Ballet shoes: tight. So tight and revealing. It was just like my foot was on the floor but my toes were all bound together.

JIM BORSTELMANN: Give me a jazz shoe. Now that's a shoe! But ballet? Eh. I looked like Little Lord Fauntleroy. And those bows—what do you do with those?

LUIS PEREZ: That little bow on those Russian boater ballet shoes felt so sissy. Then I noticed that the other guys would tuck the bow in, but when I did that, it made a blister on the top of my foot. So I'd take it back out, but when I looked in the mirror, all I saw was a sissy again. Maybe it was because I had sewn the elastic way up past my instep. By the time I got to the Joffrey, I wore canvas slippers. I'd tear out the insole to make it more flexible, soak them in fabric softener overnight, rinse them, put them on, fold down the heel, and then cross-stitch the elastics. I had many pairs, all scientifically rigged to how they would look best on my feet.

Fashion trends will change in the dance world, just as they do in normal life. Where years ago a dancer wouldn't dream of wearing a pair of tights with a run, some nowadays rip them up on purpose. Go to New York with your standard, acceptable clothing and then, as you get used to a studio, look around. If you like a particular trend and it looks good on you, by all means feel free to try it out, but don't feel pressured to keep up with the crowd. Some trends tend to make a mockery of our profession and are just plain slovenly. My rule is to dress down no more than 10 percent as I would for an audition. Look in the mirror and remember your primary purpose for taking class—to improve your technique. If the reflection is that of a dedicated dancer who just may be noticed, you are on the right track.

What to Wear to an Audition

When I was in college and auditioned for summer stock I knew I dressed with the appropriate mix of decorum and flair simply by comparing myself to the other people auditioning. I always got offers so I knew I was on the right track. Then after immersing myself in ballet and modern companies for a number of years I somehow forgot how to dress. For my first theatrical audition back in New York I wore a black cap-sleeved leotard, pink tights, tan character heels, and had my hair wrenched back in a tight bun. For my song I sang "Impossible" from *Cinderella* in a key so high I'd need to suck helium to reach the notes. Impossible is right. Impossible and wrong, wrong, wrong.

BEBE NEUWIRTH: You have to get in the game. You can't dress like a ballerina and expect someone to take you seriously as a musical theatre performer. But don't try to be someone other than who you are. Going to auditions, you see all these girls who look a certain way and get kept. It can be very tempting to put on a padded bra or cut your hair in a certain way or take on the mannerisms of someone else. I think that is self-defeating. If you get a job presenting yourself as someone else, do you have to look and behave like somebody else for a long time? It's okay to dress yourself like a particular character in a show at times. When I went for my callback for *Sweet Charity* I knew they were concerned that I didn't look old or tough enough to play a dance hall hostess. So I wore big earrings, a black turtleneck that was cut out in the back, I yanked up my tights, and didn't cover the circles under my eyes. I presented myself differently, but I wasn't being somebody else. I got the part.

<u>LUIS PEREZ:</u> I didn't know anything. I thought you went into audition for a show like you audition for a dance company. So for the invited *Cats* call I wore my best dark blue unitard, my white socks up to my knees, and my white ballet shoes. I walked into the room sleek as a panther and here are all these fantastic Broadway veterans, the best of Broadway, wearing their show jazz boots and jeans and ripped up T-shirts, looking like guy-guys, and there I am as this prim and proper ballet dancer from the Joffrey. The guys looked me up and down like I was some kind of a freak—which I was!

<u>EUGENE FLEMING:</u> I'll never forget walking into the call for *A Chorus Line* and seeing all these guys—I mean the attitude of life. I was just country. I had on a royal blue jazz unitard with big bell bottoms. I couldn't tell you what I looked like, but it didn't feel real good.

There are so many styles of dance clothing, it is puzzling to figure out what to choose. Certain cuts and colors will make your body look too thick or thin, your skin too sallow, and certain styles are just plain tacky. Sure, some people expect total freedom of expression in the artistic venue of theatre, but you must dress with the sapience and respectability that this profession demands. The two tricks are to evaluate what looks good on you—not what looks good on someone else—and to choose what feels comfortable.

Before grabbing clothes off the store rack and laying down your money, honestly study your body and make a list of your good and bad points. If this is hard, enlist the help of a friend to look at you and be completely objective. (Beware: Asking a lover may put your relationship in jeopardy.) For the moment, consider yourself an object of proportions, not a person. Height is not a factor as much as how all of your pieces fit together. The things to note are the length of your neck, torso, arms, and legs; the thickness of your waist, hips, and thighs; and the size and musculature of your back, chest, and butt. Your mission is to create the longest lines possible and to draw the eye upward to the chest and downward from the neck to shoulders. The blessing of theatre is that we portray real characters so you needn't be physically ideal. However, there is a distinct difference between the curves that nature and study have given you and what is a result of too much ice cream and french fries. A well-defined body immediately says, "This body is a reflection of dance technique and the curves are a bonus."

Since males and females are so wonderfully different, I'll separate the suggestions for each gender and body type. Then, whatever ensemble you finally decide upon, wear it to class first for a trial run. Do you like how you look in the mirror? Does a strap keep falling down? Are the pants too tight or too baggy in the crotch? Is it itchy when you sweat? Does the leotard keep riding up the back or over in front? If any little thing bothers you, find a replacement. An audition is no time to be concerned about mischievous clothing, especially if it makes you afraid to move. Once you've hit the jackpot, launder the outfit and save it solely for auditions. The peace of mind is worth it.

Females

To make your legs look long, wear flesh-colored tights with any color leotard or wear black tights under a black leotard. A colored leotard with black tights worn over it is also fine. Hike your leotard above your hip-bone, high enough to make your legs look long but without it constantly slipping into the crack of your butt. Unitards are fine for women with long legs, but should be avoided by those with a long torso and short legs. With a unitard, wear a belt or elastic to define your waist.

Your leotard should enhance your upper-body features. If you have a beautiful port de bras, you can wear almost any style of sleeve. However, if your arms are short, stick to bare arms or full-length sleeves. If your biceps and triceps are jiggly, wear sleeves long enough to bind them in. If your neck is short, wear a V-neck leotard with long or three-quarter-length sleeves. Square-cut necklines look good on most people unless you are very bony and angular. A scoop neck works well as long as you are not too busty. Pinning the scoop to make a V tends to make your cleavage prettier and your breasts less packed in. Most types of crisscross or wrap fronts look good on all types of bodies and the cut enhances your breasts while it slims your waist. The only styles to be wary of are turtlenecks and halters. Both can make your neck look short and your torso long. Of course there are exceptions. If you have a high waist, long legs, slim hips, and a long neck, you can wear a turtleneck with ease. If your back is beautifully broad, a halter will show off this terrific aspect of your physique.

Another style of dress that is attractive is tights and trunks with a form-fitting top, midriff, small T-shirt, or a button-down blouse that is tied below the breasts or at the waist. The trunks should be high-cut, preferably above your hipbones. If you only have the low-cut, pull the waistband of the trunks up, put on an elastic belt, fold the waistband over the elastic down past your hipbones, and then roll or tuck the waistband under the leg openings at each hipbone. The style of top should be chosen with the same enhancement features as listed for a leotard—sleeve length, neckline, and so on. Midriffs and shirts tied under your breasts are terrific if you have a flat stomach or good stomach muscles, but be sure you are not exposing a blubbery waist or a poochy lower stomach. The only downfall to midriffs is if the dance combination includes any body slides on the floor or you are asked to perform any partnering. In the first case, you might get a floor burn. In the second case, your skin may be slippery when being lifted. If your partner's hands slip up your rib cage, you may end up showing more than your talent.

Thongs are popular in aerobic classes and health clubs, but they purposely emphasize the bulk of your butt so unless you want the attention drawn there, I would avoid them. There is a distinct difference between looking strongly feminine and looking too much like a weight lifter. The characters that women portray onstage tend toward sexy, sassy, elegant, beautiful types. Aerobic clothing slots you into an athletic category and could possibly work against your versatility.

Wearing a padded or push-up bra is your own choice. If you are extremely flat and very self-conscious about it, a small amount of padding to tastefully augment your size may give you more self-confidence. Be forewarned that even if you are averse to a padded bra, a future costume designer will most likely stick one on you, so you might as well get used to dancing in one now. No matter your chest size, wear some sort of bra to avoid unchoreographed movement.

The colors you choose should enhance your face and hair, and shouldn't be at odds with your makeup tones. This is a very personal decision, but if you are really stuck, think opposites. Dark hair and skin look great with bright, rich colors. Fair complexions and hair handle dark colors well. No color should be so vibrant it washes you out. But there is no hard-and-fast rule. The important thing is that you feel like the color is your second skin and kin to your personal taste.

MAMIE DUNCAN-GIBBS: For my first audition I was dressed all wrong. Once I started auditioning more, I tried to figure out the types they were keeping. I found a red leotard that worked well for me and wore beige tights. That became my audition outfit.

JOANN M. HUNTER: My dance teacher said that to audition in New York you have to wear something bright to separate yourself from other people. I did it for a while but I no longer believe that. When I give auditions I don't look at what they're wearing unless I personally like it and think, "Ooo, that's cute," or if they are a slob or have no makeup on. It's the talent that counts, not the color. What if a dancer wears red, white, and blue and is a bad dancer? Sure, she'll stand out, but she'll look even worse.

If accessories are your bag, wear whatever you want as long as they don't fly up and bonk you in the face, jingle-jangle, or hurt someone else. Small earrings look really nice, some women like to tie a scarf or chain around their waist, and many wear delicate neck chains or wrist and ankle bracelets. None of these things are necessary unless they comfortably match your fashion sense.

Males

While tights are not forbidden, most men wear pants to an audition. There are two types of pants that work well for men: jazz pants and tailored street pants. The jazz pants show more of the musculature of your legs and butt, whereas the street pants can give you a longer line. If your legs are long, you can get away with either look, but if your legs are short, very thin, or you are long waisted, street pants are better because you can employ more tricks to mask your proportions. For example, the outer seam of tailored pants draws the eye toward the upper body, and the pants can be worn above the waist with suspenders or a thick belt. The fullness of the pant leg will make a thin leg appear more substantial. If you choose street pants, they should be khaki colored, black, or another subtle dark color. Pinstripes in the style of the 1930s and '40s look terrific. Stay away from plaids or bright colors or you risk looking like a costumed clown. Be sure you can move freely without the pants being too baggy in the crotch. If you choose jazz pants, consider the bulk of your thighs and buttocks, and the length of ankle to knee in relation to the length of your thigh. If your thighs are very muscular or long in comparison to your calf, choose a pant leg that falls loosely from the hip or bottom of your thigh muscle to gain the illusion of length. If your legs are muscular but are well proportioned, tighter fitting jazz pants are fine and often considered sexy.

With either pant style, you can wear T-shirts, polo shirts, tank tops, or vests with no shirt beneath. With street pants you can also wear a button-down shirt as long as you roll up the sleeves and make sure the shoulder seam doesn't droop too far down onto the upper arm to give you a slouched look. T-shirts cut at the midriff look great as long as your stomach muscles are ripped and your chest isn't sunken. Leotard tops are fine as long as they don't look too classical or academic. The more they resemble form-fitting street wear, the better. The sleeve style should enhance and expose the musculature of your shoulder and arm, whether you are lean or pumped up. Normally, short sleeves, high cap sleeves, and no sleeves are your best bet, but never a full-length. Whatever shirt you choose, tuck it smoothly and snugly into your dance belt. Only those with too much belly wear their shirts hanging out.

TOMMY TUNE: At auditions on Broadway I started being smart because I kept getting typed out a lot due to my height. I just didn't belong. So I would wear horizontal stripes up top and I would pinch down into my rib cage to lose a couple of inches. Then I wouldn't fight for the downstage position but would dance upstage where I looked smaller and I'd group myself with the taller guys. I started getting jobs, like *Baker Street.* I don't think the choreographer realized how tall I was until the first day of rehearsal. She was going along looking at her choices and suddenly, I was really way up there. I had fudged it in the audition.

Any accessories you wear should look like something that you wear every day. Many men have pierced ears and wear neck and wrist jewelry. As long as it doesn't distract or hurt you or anyone else, it's fine. Nose, navel, and nipple rings are preferably left at home, not because of their look, but because a wayward hand in a crowded room could accidentally rip them out. Bandanas and headbands work well, but stay away from baseball caps or other hats no matter how popular they may be. Too often they fly off, causing you, and all around you, to lose concentration.

The main image you want to present is, on the one hand, athletic and energetic as if you could boyishly pop up a double tour or roguishly toss dice, and on the other hand, elegantly partner a woman with sensuality and strength. This image is not weighed by the size of your biceps, but by a suggestion of strength. A lean body dressed in khakis and showing a sinewy forearm from a rolled shirt sleeve is just as attractive as the skin-tight black-clad gladiator. If in doubt, understate your clothing and avoid outlandish colors and vogue classroom styles. You don't want to risk a job for a fashion statement.

GRACIELA DANIELE: Your eye always goes to the person who is properly dressed, but it really doesn't matter as long as they are not dirty and I can see their bodies. It is my job to observe through the layers to the talent. If they have blue hair or earrings and are terrific performers then they will be good for me. Their dress is a personal taste that has nothing to do with their talent. Sometimes a kooky personality is exactly what I need. Besides, the designers are going to dress them in the show; they won't have the spiked hair. I don't care because I know I will change them.

For both men and women, the more informed you are about the show being cast, the more you can pick and choose what to wear. Read the breakdowns of the principal characters and the description of the show. Let's say the show takes place in the sugarcane fields of a hot, steamy island and one of the main characters is a cruel field boss. I'd glean that at some point the ensemble will be the poor, suffering workers, showing lots of sweaty skin. To wear a 1930s tapper outfit would look ridiculous.

Yet, if the audition call was for *42nd Street*, shorts and midriffs for the women and slacks and shirts for the men would be perfect. If the audition is a replacement call or a revival, see the show or check out the photos outside the theatre and on the CD. You can suggest the style and period of the show in your audition outfit, as long as you don't look costumed. No sequins, spangles, feathers, tuxedo jackets, or straw hats will earn you serious consideration.

JIM BORSTELMANN: I heard there was a white cat in *Cats* so I came to the audition dressed in white. All in white! White shoes, tights, leotard—the works. Who knew the white cat was played by a girl?

Proper dressing is a matter of objectivity and preference. The more honest you are about recognizing your physical fine points and flaws, the more you will enhance your image, both for yourself as you daily stand in front of a wall of mirrors in class, and in the eyes of casting people during an audition. If you dislike a color or style, don't wear it even if it's the rage. Your self-esteem and comfort far outweigh fashion.

CHAPTER EIGHT

Life Shrinks to a Look and a List: Pictures and Resumes

The function of a head shot for a dancer can be summed up in two little words: REMEMBER ME??? When an audition ends, you leave behind your calling card—your face, your contact number, and whatever experience can fit on an 8 × 10 rectangle. Years ago when everybody knew everybody else, pictures weren't very important.

GRACIELA DANIELE: I didn't have to audition much. I was very lucky in that sense. Once I got with Michael Bennett, he took me from show to show. I never even needed a head shot. I did have to audition for *Chicago*. Bobby called me at home to say he was inviting a few ladies in to audition. But it wasn't about my picture. It was about my talent.

CHITA RIVERA: I never had a professional picture until . . . Gee, I don't think I even had one for *West Side*. We, in person, were our resumes in those days.

When you become known by choreographers and casting directors, this wonderfully respectful intimacy may happen, but the reality is that today's Broadway is ever more full of new producers and investors who import directors and choreographers who may not have grown up on the Broadway beat. As well known as you may become, these new kids on the block who are in charge will want to see an accurate photo. With that in mind, let's consider what type of photograph you need strictly for a dance audition and how to create a resume.

Pictures

A photo shoot is the antithesis of a dance audition. In a photographer's studio your hair is groomed, blown, and sprayed, your face is beaten with makeup to enhance your features, your head is tilted nanometers to best capture the light, and perspiration, if any, is sucked into a tissue faster than a blink. After the shoot, the photographer brushes away any additional flaws that were magnified by the camera. The pampering and the procedure are totally correct. We're talking a close-up from the chest up. That's a lot of face, baby.

However, in a dance audition a triple pirouette is the closest you'll come to blowing your hair, your makeup will melt into rivulets of sweat, and under fluorescent or stage worklights every flawed feature will pop out to say hello. Of course, you will enter the audition well-groomed and the choreographer will know that eventually stage makeup will hide that insistent zit. But for the audition process, the trick is to find a happy marriage between your photograph and the living, breathing, sweating, not-so-perfect you.

A good head shot is pleasant and natural with no false, cutesy poses. Your eyes should sparkle and seem to say, "Not only will you love work-ing with me, I am a great friend." The professional quality of your pic-ture represents your integrity. Your mother may be a whiz with her new digital camera, but she can't compete with a professional's lighting, pho-tographic equipment, and expertise. Above all, your picture should reflect you on a good day; a look that you can re-create without plastic surgery. The temptation may be to doll up like a magazine model, but if the picture doesn't resemble the real you, it's useless. I once made the mistake of spending a great deal of money for a six-hour photo shoot where I was molded into an alien. They cut and coiffed my hair, painted my face like a piece of delicate porcelain, dressed me in their choice of clothes for the right texture, and posed me until my cheeks cramped—both sets, if you get my drift. The resulting head shots were lovely, yes, but light-years away from the real me.

The reality of an audition is that you are one of hundreds of hopefuls. As unique as we are, individuality wears thin as the audition process lumbers over hours, days, and weeks. Your photo should function as a reminder to the casting people. The worst scenario that can happen to you is this: At the end of a long audition day, the director, choreographer, and casting director wearily review their choices. Their eyeballs feel like boiled eggs and their minds are a second away from total meltdown. The casting director says, "How about D. Dancer?"

"Which one was that?" grumble the director and choreographer.

The casting director produces your head shot from one of the many piles littering the table. They stare at the photo without hint of recognition, and then flip to your resume for a clue. The choreographer and director shrug. A quick look at your audition card reveals the information: Dance 2+; Voice okay; Cute. They flip back to your face totally baffled.

"D. Dancer wore a black leotard," the casting director adds to jog their memories. Of course, three hundred and two people also wore black.

One of three responses now happens: One, they toss your photo into the trash and utter the death knell, "If we can't remember, D. Dancer couldn't have been that good." Two, they smother your photo in the pile marked "Second Choice"—a heap that gets reviewed only in extreme desperation. Three, they feel magnanimous and say, "Well, if you think so, bring D. Dancer back in and we'll take another look." Don't bank on number three. Most likely, you have lost your callback because your picture misrepresented you.

MAMIE DUNCAN-GIBBS: For my first audition in New York I didn't have a picture, only a resume. It was for a cruise ship. Out of two hundred girls, I made it down to the last ten. They said that they were going to call in the next few days to let us know what was going on. I didn't have an answering machine back then so I stayed home for three whole days. Then I realized they weren't going to call. I wondered if they even remembered me.

There is a big difference in the timing of when pictures are collected for a dance audition as opposed to commercials, television, and film. In an open Equity dance call, pictures are not collected until after the casting people have seen you dance. There is no sense having photos of people who may be cut on the first combination. Once you are asked to stay to dance further or to sing, the casting people will want to see your picture and resume. (If you attend an invited call, your picture and resume will already have been submitted to the casting people in order to secure an appointment.) On the other hand, for commercials, television, and film the usual procedure to gain an audition is for you or your agent to submit your picture first. If your look is right, you will then get a chance to show your talent.

Therefore, the type of photograph for each venue is different. Commercial producers usually want a clean-cut, all-American type to sell their products. Daytime dramas (soaps) tell the intimate stories of beautiful people, so an upscale, more glamorous photo is best. For film, the glamour shot or a legitimate theatre shot can work. These venues are terrific to earn money and to further your career. Eventually, you will need all of these varied photos to get your foot in the door. But for now, all you need is a professional head shot that looks like you.

You may question whether you should get a traditional head shot from the shoulders up, or a mid-shot taken from the waist or hips up. More and more, people are using these mid-shots. The advantage is that they are a reminder not only of your face, but also of your body. After all, in a dance audition the focus is on the complete person. However, taking a successful mid-shot takes more time and often more money. The background becomes a significant factor and the pose must look natural. Do you wear street clothes so you can use the picture for theatre and film, or do you wear dance clothes? The dance clothes look is fine for theatre, but it may type you out for a film call. My suggestion is that if you don't have the finances to fiddle around, aim for a head shot.

Once you have your photo session and receive the master sheet, ask the photographer which photos are more outstanding in his opinion and show the sheet to numerous friends or your agent, if you have one. When we look at our reflections in the mirror we tend to focus on certain virtues or flaws, and rarely see ourselves as others see us. The same goes for photos. We tend to pick out what we want to see, rather than which picture best represents us. In turn, while you may obsess about your dimples, you may miss the fact that the lighting is not as good as in another shot. An outsider views the entire photo and matches its quality with what you really look like to the outside world.

For those of you coming from a dance company, save your dance shots for your living room wall. Your dancing will be judged in the flesh. Getting head shots may seem foreign to you, but it's a professional sign that you understand the conventions of Broadway. One time I was handed a girl's photo in which she was facing three-quarters away from the camera in a piqué attitude. All I could see of her head was the back of her ear and a beaded bun. When later looking over the pictures, I couldn't remember what her face looked like for the life of me. Also, the photo was so balletic, I appreciated the training, but questioned more than usual whether she was versatile in theatre dance. What good is that type of negative attention?

Another caution is that casting people assume you have hundreds of photos. Once you hand one to them, it belongs to them. After all, the hope is that if you aren't right for this particular job, they will keep your picture on file for a replacement call or another show.

LUIS PEREZ: I didn't have a regular picture and resume. Much to my regret, I gave them all these original production photos from the Joffrey, thinking I would get them back. I never did.

Finding a photographer is not a problem. For your first step you need not go any further than the many fine photographers who are credited for the head shots in this book. There are many other photographers who advertise in the trade papers, magazines, and on callboards. Logging on to www.backstage.com and entering the performer's resource directory will lead you to many sites where you can view portfolios and compare prices.

Cost of Pictures

Getting head shots is kind of like going out to eat. You can grab the eighty-nine-cent breakfast special at the corner deli, lunch at a moderate café for twenty bucks, or dine at a five-star restaurant where every bite adds five dollars to your bill. In each case you receive a varying amount of frills and pampering, and in each you take your chances. A high cost doesn't necessarily guarantee satisfaction; the bacon and egg on a roll wrapped in foil just may surpass the New Zealand quail marinated in curry and grilled with skin of newt. With photos, you may pay through the nose for a full-day affair or choose the bargain deal, and in each case, end up with stunners or zilch.

Photograph sessions range from $99 for a Head Shot Special to over $800 for many set-ups, makeup, hair, and retouching. In some cases you

$99	One roll of film (36 shots). Second roll ranges $50–$75. One 8 × 10 head shot per roll. Some let you keep the negatives. Retouching is usually extra.
$150–$200	Two or three rolls of film. Two or three contact sheets. Two or three 8 × 10s. Sometimes base makeup is offered. Negatives may be free.
$300–$450	Three or four rolls of film. Three or four contact sheets. Three or four 8 × 10s. Some different set-ups.
$500 and up	Four rolls of film, four contact sheets, four 8 × 10s. Different set-ups—indoor/outdoor shots. Lots of time and personal attention. May be digital.

receive 8 × 10s, negatives, and free reshoots. In others, you pay for each item, like dining à la carte. The table above shows average categories, though understand that each photographer is unique and offers variations within each category.

In most cases, hair and makeup are extra, ranging $75–$150. If the makeup/hair artist stays with you throughout the session to change your look, it costs more. Photo retouching costs around $30. (This is helpful to remove temporary problems like pimples or shadows, but don't be tempted to airbrush every line and flaw away.) Some photographers are connected with reproduction establishments so you can get a discount on bulk copies of both your pictures and resumes. Some photographers offer discounts to students, to former clients, for cash payment, and if you forego an initial interview.

JOANN M. HUNTER: I have to hire hair and makeup people. I can do it for every day or for a show, but close up, there's no way. I usually tell them I just want a commercial look, kind of happy, easy, and one that looks very much like me. Then I get a more serious, upscale look. But I always tell them to only do something with my hair that I could possibly do myself with a little work.

When choosing your photographer, there are four points to consider: your finances, how many set-ups you want, how you like the photographer's former work, and how you like the photographer personally. If you are cutting costs, I suggest you aim strictly for a good head shot that will suffice for theatre auditions. If you can afford only $99, take a good look at the photographer's work. Is the lighting harsh? Are the poses natural? Would you want to hire the people in the photographs? With only one roll of film you can't afford experimentation. Be as prepared as possible with your clothes, hair, and makeup. Bring your makeup, hair products, and blow dryer, just in case you get grubby on your way to the studio. Ask the photographer for clothing suggestions when you set up the appointment, and, above all, in the session be as relaxed as possible. You don't want to waste the first ten shots loosening up. Of course, the more set-ups you can afford, the better. But again, do your homework on the photographer's former work. A high price doesn't necessarily mean you agree with the photographer's creative approach. Remember, you are out to capture an image of the real you, not an artsy-fartsy picture that belongs in a coffee-table book.

It is worth the time, or lack of discount, to meet the photographer before agreeing on a session. You need to feel totally comfortable in front of the camera. All photographers mean well, but tastes differ. If music plays, do you like the style? Is this a person who makes you want to feel intimate with the camera? I have been with some photographers who are dreams for my personality, and others who make me feel like a caddy at their exclusive golf club. Their work may be great, but if you don't feel at home, your chances of having a selection of good photos from which to choose will be limited.

In reproducing your photos, you have choices of matte or glossy, with or without a border, and with or without your name. Typically for each one hundred copies, a border costs about $25, name $8.50, photos $55 to $65, and negatives about $16. If your photographer gives you the negatives, you save money at the reproduction house. Be sure to ask if you can bring your own negatives. Some reproduction houses insist on making their own negatives. Although names and borders look nice, they are not mandatory, so feel free to keep your expenses lower by foregoing the frills.

If you really can't afford to hire a photographer, you can try your luck with having a friend take pictures of you. Submitting some kind of picture at an audition is better than no picture at all, though its amateur quality will be noted, especially by casting directors. Go this route if you must, but make saving for professional head shots a number-one goal. Your picture should not be an apology for your lack of professionalism.

<u>Eugene Fleming</u>: My uncle took my first head shot. We went to some waterfall in Virginia. I had on a black-and-white pinstripe suit with a flower in the lapel. At that point I had little sideburns. I was cool. Wouldn't you know, years later I was in Michael Bennett's office and, as a joke, he had a wall of head shots that were all wrong. There I was, leaning against the waterfall looking like a pimp. And the worst part about it was my shot was in color. All the black-and-white pictures and then there's one in color—yours truly.

On a final note, remember that you will pay for a series of head shots throughout the years as your look changes. One day you may finally decide to shave or grow the beard, drastically restyle the hair, or get that nose job. If physical changes are imminently on your mind, don't waste money on an expensive photo session until you are satisfied and comfortable with the new you. As for maturing, time does not stand still. Keep your picture up to date as those wonderful character lines invade your visage.

Resumes

One of the greatest fears of a performer new to the New York scene is not having a sizeable resume. The fact is, something has to be on it so that the casting people can connect to your experience. Don't worry if you can't list ten Broadway shows. Look carefully instead at what accomplishments you *have* made. As long as you have consistently studied or performed regionally, you will be able to compile a legitimate resume with pride. See if any of the following areas pertain to you.

College

Casting directors do not expect college students to have extensive professional musical theatre training. Most are familiar with the curriculums of the performing arts colleges, so the name will speak for itself. List a sampling of your performances in school productions, citing roles if applicable. Under "Training" list your major and any non-dance classes like acting or voice, if they were not a part of your normal schedule. If any productions were directed or choreographed by outside professionals, be sure to list the name.

Dance Companies

No one will cast aspersion on the training you receive by being in a dance company. All companies perform, so you automatically have stage experience. The type of company—ballet, jazz, modern, and so on—will reflect the style in which you have most immersed yourself. If the company's repertoire was varied, list a sampling of diverse pieces you performed in and indicate the name of the role or position—soloist, principal, or corps. Definitely list under "Training" your voice teacher because the biggest question will be whether or not you can sing. If your company was strictly one style of dance, list whatever other styles you study and with whom. If guest choreographers came in to set any of the pieces, list the name.

Dinner, Stock, and Regional Theatre

State the name of the production, your role, and where you performed. If a well-known performer, director, choreographer, or producer was connected with the show, let it be known. This reflects the quality of the production, or separates which particular version of *The Music Man* you were in. If the show is new, list the writer and director or choreographer. Include under "Training" your various dance, voice, and acting classes to show that you study as well as perform.

Workshops and Showcases

To develop projects without a huge cash outlay, many producers finance workshops. At the end of the workshop, presentations are made to investors. There is no guarantee that the show will collect enough revenue to realize a full-blown production, but that does not diminish your participation. List the name of the show, your position, and the director, choreographer, and creators if you have room. Showcases are low-budget, limited-run productions. The intent of raising money is the same as a workshop, but the production is fully realized onstage with a paying audience. List the name of the showcase, your position, the name of the theatre, and the choreographer or director.

Staged Readings

The creators of a show—the writer, composer, and lyricist—need to hear their work out loud to assess its potential. A staged reading is a bare-bones presentation with no lights or costumes and the staging usually consists of sitting, standing, and switching podiums. The actors may be familiar with the piece, but they hold their scripts. Participating in a staged reading means that you act or sing well enough to carry the show without benefit of theatrical augmentation. List the name of the reading, your role, and the director.

Industrials

Until you have so much theatre experience on your resume you need to write "Industrials—list upon request" to save room, list the name of the industrial, your role, the choreographer or director, and the production company. Where you performed is not necessary. We all know industrials usually go to resorts with really big swimming pools.

Film

Feature films, independent films, and movies made for television often have dance sequences. List the title, its venue, and the director and choreographer. If you have a straight part, list the character name. If you are in a student film, list the director or choreographer and the school under whose tutelage it was filmed. Regarding work as an extra in film, list the name of the film, state whether you were simply an extra or performed as a dance extra, and list the director or choreographer. As your resume builds remove the extra work. While it is a noble profession, its inclusion on a dance resume is mostly to fill space.

Music Videos

List the name of the video, the musical group or vocal artist, your role, and the choreographer. If you are featured, let it be known. Dancers in videos do not receive screen credit as they do in film.

Theme Parks

List the name of your revue and your role—dancer, featured dancer, lead singer, and so forth, not Goofy or the third Little Pig. These character names conjure up images of people in heavy costumes handing out candy and posing for pictures with squirming toddlers. However, if you played Cinderella or Captain Hook where your acting abilities weren't buried under fifty pounds of costume, list the role. State which theme park and the choreographer. If you happened to work there three summers in a row, write, "Summer '97, '98, '99."

Cruise Ships

List the name of the cruise line or ship, your position, and the choreographer. You needn't list the names of the revues because most people know that the same group performs various shows to keep the passengers amused. However, if you have created your own act, or if a show is a cut-down version of a Broadway musical, let it be known. Many performers start their professional careers on cruise ships so it is a very valid credit. Besides, for those of us who have choreographed for cruise ships, we sympathize with living below deck in windowless compartments and performing on a rollicking stage. It builds experience, fortitude, and a really strong stomach.

Cabaret and Nightclub Revues

List the name of the revue, your role, and where it was done. Use common sense here. If the revue was at the Tropicana in Las Vegas, list both the hotel name and the city. If you played the back lounge at the Sleep-If-You-Dare Motel on the outskirts of Boise, just write something akin to "Name That Tune Revue—featured dancer—Bobby Be-Bop, choreographer." Leave it up to the casting people to ask if they want to know more.

Contests, Competitions, and Scholarships

Anybody can enter a dance contest so list these only if you have won one of the top three prizes. State the name of the competition, your prize, and where it was held. If the competition or scholarship is a pretty big deal like the Bob Fosse Scholarship Award or an International Ballet

Competition, it can warrant its own line. If it is a beauty or body pageant, put your winning status under "Special Skills." Being Miss North Dakota or Mr. Muscles is an accomplishment, but it doesn't mean you can dance.

Choreographer's Audition

In order for a producer or director to determine which choreographer to choose for a show, many ask that various new choreographers put together one or more numbers from the show. (A well-known choreographer already has a track record.) Since this is a relatively new practice, the situations vary, but the common denominator is that the choreographer asks or hires dancers to work on the numbers required. List the name of the show, indicating that it is a Choreographer's Audition, your role, and the name of the choreographer. Ha ha—you thought performers were the only ones who have to audition.

Special Events

Let's say your marching band or cheerleading squad performed during halftime at the Rose Bowl. If you haven't much theatrical experience to list, its inclusion on your resume shows that your group was chosen to be on national TV, you have performed in front of a large crowd, and have an expertise other than formal dance. But don't stretch these events too far. Performing at the Kiwanis Club picnic on Memorial Day is a no-no. It is far wiser to list your baton twirling, musical instrument, or champion yo-yo abilities under "Special Skills."

Hospitals, Nursing Homes, Mall Openings

Forget it. As altruistic as these performances are, you can't use them unless you are a preteen. Instead, use the name of the dance group, the city, and the name of the director.

I have been very repetitive with the instructions to include the names of the choreographers, directors, or stars of your productions if the show itself is not common knowledge. When perusing your resume, the casting people are searching for any clue they can relate to, anyone whose work they know, anyone they can call for a recommendation. The theatre is a small world where people work together in the most unlikely places over the years. It is also a world where the same shows are done over and over. Narrowing down the specifics helps the print on your resume take on a life.

GRACIELA DANIELE: Where dancers' resumes are concerned, I look a lot at the training—where they studied, what dance vocabulary. I think that is important, apart from the shows they've done.

If you haven't much of the above to include on your resume, the temptation is to lie. My opinion is, don't do it. The odds are you will get caught, look like a fool, and probably won't get the job. Personally I caught one girl in a rather creative lie and it soured me against her. The audition was for a small regional theatre production where the singing audition came before the dance audition. Before this particular girl sang, I noticed on her resume that she had worked on a new production at another regional theatre and had played the part of "Paige Turner." By coincidence, I had been the assistant choreographer on the production and knew that she wasn't in the cast, nor was there a character named "Paige Turner." I asked her about the show and rather evilly let her dig herself deeper into her grave of lies. Then I let the bomb drop that I had worked on the show. She turned into cherry Jell-O and explained that she had been a production assistant. During the run of the show, she had indeed been a page turner—the girl who turned the pages of the script to cue any actor who forgot their lines. I told her to go ahead and sing, but the poor thing could hardly get a note out through her humiliation.

Had she told the truth about being a production assistant, I would have been in her court on two counts. One, I appreciate how hard production assistants work in regional theatres. The hours and demands can be grueling. Two, in order to make her feel more at ease, I would have chatted awhile about the production. Her lie burned our common bond.

If you have talent, you will eventually get hired. It is far better to audition for small productions where your credits aren't expected to be overwhelming than to lie. You will build your experience, your contacts, and your resume.

TOMMY TUNE: I don't think there's any reason to lie on a resume. Just tell the truth and sometimes the truth is that you played Such-and-Such in Mrs. So-and-So's Diction School. That's sort of charming because you know it's the truth. The truth is great. And you never get in trouble saying the truth because then you don't have to remember what your lie was. I lied to an agent once in L.A. They asked if I could do a split and I said that I could, even though I could only do a jazz split. There was this one joke thing in a sitcom and I was a hippie and I had to go, "Man, I gotta split!" and then fall into a split. It would have been fabulous, but I couldn't do it. I got paid, but I thought, "I'm never going to lie again."

Since lying on a resume is such a subjective area, I present the other end of the spectrum. After all, you are in New York where competition is the name of the game and show business is truly a business.

JOANN M. HUNTER: I lied on my resume because I didn't know what else to do. It's not like I went to college so I could list some school experience. I had nothing except Opryland. So I made up shows or I looked in *Back Stage* or *Showbiz*, figured out when they were happening, and then wrote that I did them. I never got caught, except for one close call. I put Jerry Robbins down as director of the *West Side Story* I did in 1985 when it was really directed by Ruth Mitchell. When I later auditioned for *Jerome Robbins' Broadway* I forgot to fix it. Jerry looked at me and said, "JoAnn, when and who did you do *West Side* with?" I went, "You. You came in for the last part." I was telling the truth because he had, but—phew! The more I worked, I would erase one show at a time until it all became true. Except for my height and weight. I took those off completely. Nobody needs to know that.

ROBERT MONTANO: It's tough when you start in this business because you have no resume. So I made one up and padded the shit out of it: I did *Guys and Dolls* at the Jewish Temple in Ohio . . . Not! I learned that in the beginning when I admitted I had no experience, they didn't take a second glance, but when I lied and gave them something to look at, they gave me the time of day. But I never put characters that I couldn't play and I made sure I knew the character in the show so it was plausible. And I would never, ever put understudy because understudies are so valuable that once they see it on your resume, forget it. You're done.

You're now an understudy in that show. My only advice about this is, don't get caught.

If you really feel you need to, take your chances. But before you lie, consider the following audition possibilities. They are but a sampling.

1. The musical director asks you to sing another song and you don't have one. He looks at your resume and says, "I see you played Ado Annie in *Oklahoma!* Sing 'I'm Just a Girl Who Can't Say No.'" Gulp . . . Do you know it?

2. The choreographer says, "Wow. I've heard about that production. What finally happened with the stage?" Sweat . . . Do you know that the turntable totally failed and all of you dancers had to haul it around and around?

3. The director says, "My lover played the lead in that show." Yikes . . . Do you know the lover's name? Will the director ask about you over martinis tonight?

4. They all commiserate about working at the Dastardly Playhouse in Wisconsin at one time or other then turn to you and ask, "And where did you have to sleep while you were there?" Um . . . in the back bedroom of my long-lost aunt?

Do you really want to risk it?

EUGENE FLEMING: Back when I first started I had some stuff on my resume that I made up. And then as I started to accumulate shows, the lies started coming off. I don't think I ever got caught, but I do remember one time someone saying, "Did you? Were you in that? Are you sure you did that show?" It wasn't a great feeling.

Cost of Resumes

The more you create and copy resumes yourself, the more money you will save. If you don't have your own computer or word processor, ask your friends. Years ago not every household even had a typewriter, but today PCs are as common as telephones. You don't need to type sixty words a minute or be a computer whiz. Patience and the old hunt-and-peck method are just fine.

If you find setting up margins, centering, tabbing, and actually typing too daunting a task, hesitate before you hire a professional service. Chances are the friend who owns a computer knows how to type and may appreciate being paid a third of the cost of a professional, or better yet, will do it for free. Write out the information very clearly in the exact format of a resume. (See the following section, "How to Write a Resume.") A good idea is to provide a floppy disk so that you can store the resume. That way, later additions and omissions can be entered in a matter of minutes. Print out a copy and you're set to head to the copy store.

If no one you know in Manhattan owns a computer, send the information to someone at home. For the cost of a stamp, mail the handwritten resume and then have the person send the typed version back in a manila envelope so it doesn't get creased. For less than a dollar and in about a week, you've got a clean resume that can be copied. Again, be very specific about the format since you won't be sitting with them while they type it up.

Many large office-supply establishments provide self-service copy machines for about six cents a copy. Therefore, one hundred copies will cost you six dollars. Copying establishments typically charge about nine cents a copy for one hundred resumes. By taking a little extra time, you save three dollars by doing it yourself. Remember that the resume must fit on the back of an 8 × 10 picture. Normal paper is 8½ × 11. Many photocopying stores reduce the resume for a minimal additional cost when copying in bulk. This cost for reduction averages around seven dollars. You can keep the seven dollars in your pocket if you scissor the resumes down yourself or use the office-supply stores that provide self-serve paper cutters for free to customers who use their self-serve copying machines. If you decide to spring for professional reduction of your resume, take note that the print will also be reduced. No casting director wants to struggle through teeny-tiny print so plan your initial font carefully.

Shop around for the best deal both in self-serve and professional copying establishments. Don't feel the need to be fancy with layouts and quality of paper. Casting people want to read who you are, what you've done, where you study, and if you have any special skills as quickly as possible. At this point in your career, give them the information in an accurate, clear manner and save your pennies.

How to Write a Resume

The mechanics of writing a resume are quite simple.

1. Set the margins so you can fit in as much information as possible on an 8 × 10 piece of paper. This is very important if you are using a computer since the default setting for margins is usually one inch at the top and bottom and one and a quarter on the sides. You don't need that much white empty space, except if you want to mask a skimpy resume.

2. Center your name at the top in a larger print than the rest of the text.

3. On the next line center your union affiliates, if you have any.

4. Drop down a line or two and on the left, list your telephone number and service. If you have representation, only the agent or manager's number needs to be listed. Don't write down your address. Unlike other businesses where you may be notified of acceptance through a letter, theatre conducts its business over the phone. Also, many people see your resume, perhaps even the trash man, I hate to say. You don't want anyone getting ideas. A weird phone call can be dealt with; a weirdo waiting for you beside your front door is another story.

5. Directly across on the right, list your height, weight, hair, and eye color. If you know and are confident of your vocal range, write either the name (such as lyric baritone, soprano) or your actual note range, low to high.

6. Let the lists begin.

Normally your resume is divided into three columns, and as many of these sections as pertain to you in descending order: Broadway, National Tours, Off-Broadway, Regional, Workshops and Showcases, Film, Television, Dance Companies, Industrials, Commercials, Education or Training, Special Skills. If you do not have enough to warrant separate sections, lump categories together in a logical, clear manner. For example, "Theatrical Experience" includes any show or play that is not on Broadway. Be creative with print size and spacing so nothing is bunched up. The fewer credits you have, the more you can spread the information out. Look at the following fabricated examples of resume formats.

YOUR NAME
AEA SAG

Agent:	Harry Helper		Height:
Tel:	212-000-0000		Weight:
			Hair:
			Eyes:

Broadway

NAME OF SHOW	Chorus	Name of Theatre
NAME OF SHOW	Chorus, u/s role	Name of Theatre

National Tours

NAME OF SHOW	Character name	
NAME OF REVIVAL	Swing, dance captain	Director, star, or year

Off-Broadway

NAME OF SHOW	Featured dancer	Name of Theatre
NAME OF SHOW	Chorus	Name of Theatre

Regional and Stock

NAME OF SHOW	Character name	Name of Theatre, director
NAME OF SHOW	Chorus	Name of Dinner Theatre, starring
NAME OF SHOW	Chorus, u/s character	Producer, choreographer

Film

NAME OF FILM	Dancer	Producer
NAME OF FILM	Dancer	Director or choreographer

Television

NAME OF TV FILM	Character name	TV Network Movie of the Week
NAME OF TV PROGRAM	Dancer	TV Network, Choreographer
NAME OF TV SPECIAL	Featured Dancer	TV Network, Choreographer

Dance Companies

NAME OF COMPANY (City)	Position
NAME OF COMPANY (City)	Position

Industrials and Commercials—List upon request

Training
College
Dance studios, styles, and teachers
Voice teacher
Acting teacher

Special Skills
State champion for gymnastics, juggler, musical instrument, dialects (French, Spanish, German)

Figure 8–1. Sample resume

YOUR NAME

AEA AGMA

Tel: 201-000-0000   Height:
            212-000-0000 (service)   Weight:
                                    Hair:
                                    Eyes:
                                    Vocal range:

Theatrical Experience

NAME OF SHOW	Chorus	Name of Theatre
NAME OF SHOW	Chorus, u/s role	Name of Theatre
NAME OF SHOW	Character name	Name of Theatre, choreographer
NAME OF SHOW	Chorus	Name of Theatre, choreographer, starring

Workshops and Showcases

NAME OF WORKSHOP	Character name	Pre-B'way workshop Dir., Chor.
NAME OF SHOWCASE	Dancer	Name of Theatre, choreographer
NAME OF SHOWCASE	Character name	Name of Theatre, director
NAME OF WORKSHOP	Chorus	Name of LORT Theatre, chor.
NAME OF SHOWCASE	Chorus, u/s character	Producer, choreographer

Special Events

AIDS Benefit	Singer/Dancer	Place, choreographer
Choreographer's Audition *(NAME OF SHOW)*	Dancer	Choreographer
NAME OF SHOW	Featured dancer	Encore Series, City Center, Choreographer

Dance Companies

NAME OF COMPANY (City)	Soloist	Director, choreographer
NAME OF COMPANY (City)	Name of ballet	Choreographer
	Name of ballet	
	Name of ballet	
NAME OF COMPANY (City)	Works by Agnes DeMille, Paul Taylor, Twyla Tharp, Jose Limón	Director

Training

Dance studios, styles, and teachers
Voice teacher
Acting teacher

Special Skills

Voice-overs, fencing, karate, hip-hop, partnering, choreography

Figure 8–2. Sample resume

YOUR NAME

Tel: 201-000-0000   Height:
         212-000-0000 (service)   Weight:
                                    Hair:
                                    Eyes:

Theatrical Experience

NAME OF SHOW	Chorus	Name of Theatre
NAME OF SHOW	Chorus, u/s role	Name of Theatre
NAME OF SHOW	Character name	Name of Theatre, choreographer
NAME OF SHOW	Chorus	Name of Theatre, choreographer, starring

Scholarships/Awards

First-place winner Hellas Dance Festival	Tap	YEAR
Grand Champion Star Expo Solo Division	CITY	YEAR
NYCDA Regional Senior Outstanding Dancer Scholarship winner		YEAR

Cruise Lines and Theme Parks

NAME OF CRUISE LINE	Dancer	Choreographer
NAME OF CRUISE LINE	Lead vocalist	Musical director, choreographer
LUCY AND ETHEL	Lucy	Ocean Cruises; self-conceived and choreographed, Mus. Dir.:
NAME OF THEME PARK	Dancer	Choreographer
NAME OF THEME PARK	Emcee	Kid's Slime Show

Training
College, degree
Ballet: teacher
Jazz: teacher
Tap: teacher
Voice: teacher
Acting: teacher

Special Skills
Stage combat, runway and print model, tennis, aerobics instructor, certified dog behaviorist

Figure 8–3. Sample resume

YOUR NAME

Tel: 201-000-0000   Height:
        212-000-0000 (service)   Weight:
                                                       Hair:
                                                       Eyes:

Theatrical Experience

NAME OF SHOW	Chorus	Name of Community Theatre
NAME OF SHOW	Chorus, u/s role	Name of Dinner Theatre
NAME OF SHOW	Character name	Your college
NAME OF SHOW	Chorus	Your college, guest choreographer
NAME OF SHOW	Featured dancer	Your college
NAME OF SHOW	Character name	Your college

Industrials

NAME OF COMPUTER COMPANY	Singer/Dancer	Choreographer
NAME OF SOFT DRINK	Featured dancer	Choreographer

Training
Performing Arts High School
College, degree
Ballet: teacher
Jazz: teacher
Tap: teacher
Voice: teacher
Acting: NYC teacher
        NYC teacher

Special Skills
Dance teacher, lifeguard, piano, birdcalls, front and back walkover, 3 years volunteer U.S. Handicapped Association

Figure 8–4. Sample resume

Once your resume is cut to 8 × 10 size, attach it to the back of your picture with glue or staples in all four corners so it doesn't flap around. Never hand in your resume attached only by a paper clip or totally separated from your picture. One or the other is bound to get lost in the shuffle.

For commercials, television, and film, create a different resume. Flip credits for those venues to the top, then list your theatre credits, training, and so on. Under "Special Skills" list more of your nondance skills—expert pizza tosser, sleight of hand, licensed driver—if you can really do them.

Your resume will be in constant flux as you get more jobs. Replace the minor work with more recent theatrical experience. Don't panic that each time you get a job you need to run off one hundred new resumes. It is perfectly fine to handwrite your current job at the top of your resume. The usual wording is, "Currently in (name of show)—(name of theatre)" or "Currently playing (character name) in (name of show)—(name of theatre)."

I know of hardly anyone who is 100 percent satisfied with their pictures and resumes. We all wish for the perfect look or more credits. For each show we can list, there is another that we hadn't gotten or didn't take because it was the wrong timing. It's also the nature of the beast of dance to abhor being judged by a look and a list. What we do is live, intangible, and can't be represented in one-dimensional black and white. But these tools are the rules of the profession. Once you have them you are ready to tackle any audition with pride. You have studied, you have prepared, and you have the courage to follow your dream.

TOMMY TUNE: When I'm casting I hardly ever read resumes because I'm so into looking at what's happening onstage. When a person first walks on that stage, that's what I notice. If you don't know how to walk, learn. It's so important when you hear your name called to make an entrance with assurance. I don't even look at their pictures until after the audition when I go home to help me remember. But most of the time the pictures don't look like them anyway. It's very hard to make head shots happen. I've never had a successful head shot of me because so much of what I am is my height. And yet I worked.

CHAPTER NINE

Before the Jaws of the Beast: Preparing for an Audition

Out of all the theatre auditions on Broadway, dancers have it the hardest. Actors recite prepared monologues and singers sing prepared songs. Even if an actor has to cold read, the words are in black and white and needn't be memorized. Singers may have to dance, but only after they have shown their primary talent with a song they may have worked on for years. Both groups get individual, private time with the casting people. Dancers, on the other hand, enter a land of mystery and multitude with each audition. Within minutes you have to learn foreign combinations thrown at you faster than a speeding bullet, and then perform them with feigned ease, maximum technique, and gusto. The room may be so crowded you need a periscope to see the combination, the choreography may be perplexing, and when it's your moment in a group of three, an inconsiderate competitor may crash into you. The pressure of this situation of immediate input with immediate results is intense. Everyone on both sides of the table wishes there was a better way, but no one has found it yet. To muster the courage to face this inescapable heaven or hell, preparation and self-confidence are your best allies.

The first step of preparation is rather obvious. You have to find out which shows, Equity or non-Equity, are holding auditions. Nearly every producer worth their mettle posts the calls in the newspaper *Back Stage*. Online you will find listings at www.actorsequity.org in their casting call section, in the chat rooms of www.playbill.com, or simply by entering a search for dance auditions. At Actors' Equity on West 46th Street, the calls are posted one week in advance and a sign-up sheet provided. (Whatever number you sign up is the number of the audition card you will receive on the morning of the audition.) Doubtless you will hear news of auditions at dance studios. Once you have sifted through all the calls, schedule your week to hit whatever ones feel right for you.

I caution you to be very wary of non-Equity auditions posted in regular newspapers or online, and if you have any hesitations, bring a friend with you to check it out. When I first moved to the city I went alone to a call which seemed bona fide but must have been for strippers or call girls or I don't know what. Instead of a studio, the address led to the "producer's" office. After asking my name, this unshaven fat man stood up from behind his desk, walked over to me, and pawed my breasts saying, "You'll do." In a flash my Irish/Lithuanian anger rocketed from my toes to my fist and I hauled off and belted him in the jaw. He really got mad so I flew out of there. What makes me laugh is as I ran away he actually yelled, "You'll never work again in this town!"

Your first auditions and subsequent work may not be for a Broadway show. Frankly, there are not that many positions available. By working in national tours, regional and dinner theatres, and industrials outside of New York you will gain experience, credits, and the rent. The path for many people, including myself, was to come to New York and then go out on the road for a number of years. That's fine. You are still working in a profession you love. If you are non-Equity, this will probably be the case to gain your Equity card or to earn credits toward your Equity eligibility.* Having your Equity card is not the be-all and end-all when you

---

* The Equity Membership Candidate Program is based on accumulating work credits toward full membership in the union. When you work as a nonunion actor or stage manager at an Equity-approved participating theatre, you can register for the program. It is as simple as filling out an EMC form and paying a $100 fee. The fee is later credited toward your initiation fee when you join the union as a full member. Once you accumulate fifty weeks of work, you are eligible for full membership. Don't panic that you need to work fifty weeks in a row. The weeks can extend over any period of time. But, once you've got fifty weeks under your belt, you must sign an Equity contract if your next gig is in a Equity theatre. In other words, if you want to work in a union theatre, you've got to join the union.

are beginning. There are many well-paying non-Equity shows, tours, and variety shows holding auditions. Remember, once you get your card you can no longer perform in any non-Equity production and you need to pay your bills before you get the big break.

MAMIE DUNCAN-GIBBS: My very first job was a revue that was supposed to go to Tokyo, Singapore, and Santo Domingo. We ended up going to Fort Lauderdale instead. When we got there the theatre we were to play was boarded up and they had only given us one-way airplane tickets. I stood there and cried. The producer came and said it was a minor problem and that in two weeks we could play another theatre down there. So they put us up in a place called "Tahiti Gardens," and we rehearsed in one of the rooms. When we finally got to the theatre we found out it was an Equity house so we had to join the union. I got my card on that very first show! The only bummer was we were being paid $300 a week when we were nonunion and dropped to $225.25 which was Equity scale at that time. Plus I had to dish out the $500 initiation fee and $35 for dues. That was okay, except when I got back to New York I thought, "My God, here I am as green as a tree and now I have to audition with Broadway people."

JIM BORSTELMANN: Disney Summer Magic at Radio City Music Hall was my first job. In the ballet combination I gave them these huge sissonnes and turns, and I found out later that one of the casting directors leaned to another and said, "Who's Eddie Villella?" No one told us that they were auditioning for alligators to lift the hippos in "Fantasia." I got the job and they put this big head on me and basically said, "Leap out, alligator. Partner the hippo. Be happy." My favorite job.

In the old days, there were separate non-Equity open calls for shows—the true cattle calls. Today, however, it is a waiting game. You have to go to the Equity Chorus call and ask if they are seeing any nonunion people. Invariably, the answer will be "If there's time," meaning you have to sit and wait until the end of each segment to find out if they will see you or not. Sometimes this takes until the end of the day, sometimes a few hours, often not at all. By union law, all Equity people must be seen first. On the off-chance you do get seen, time will be short and the casting people will be tired. Buck yourself up to learn and perform as quickly as possible, without desperation. It's hard. More so than in a normal audition, your talent has to make them sit up and take notice in seconds. Do not, do not complain that you've waited all day. You are being granted a privilege.

TOMMY TUNE: When I direct and choreograph a show a lot of times I'll find much fresher, new, naïve, raw talent from the open calls. I stay for the non-Equity people at the end of the day. I've found some good ones. That's where I would've been. That's where somebody would have found me if I hadn't had that one Equity job in Dallas where I got my card before hitting Broadway.

JOANN M. HUNTER: When I was nonunion sitting in the hall with the union people, I felt inadequate. I was sure everybody knew—that instead of having a scarlet "A" on my breast like Hester Prynne, I had a big "Non-union" sign. The waiting all day—it's horrible. I don't wish it on anybody. It's a vicious circle. You can't get a job unless you are in the union and you can't get in the union unless you get a job. On the other hand, I've worked my way up in this business and I've worked hard to gain a reputation that is fairly decent. I feel I should get first dibs on a job, as much as my heart goes out to the people sitting in the hall like I had to.

The second step of preparation is to gather your gear and your guts for each audition. On the morning of an audition you'll wake up with whatever dance and vocal technique you have thus far gained. No genie is going to pop out of your toaster to grant you the three wishes of better extension, more pirouettes, or a high C. Stash any doubts you have that you won't be good enough under your pillow, and concentrate on the things you can control.

What to Pack in Your Dancebag

First and foremost, write down where and when the audition is being held or tear the item out of the newspaper. Then figure out how you are going to get there, which subway or bus, and write that down. (If you found the audition on the Actors' Equity website, you may have noticed that there is a link to Mapquest for directions.) Until you know New

York City by rote, it's easy to get streets, avenues, east, and west mixed up. Even for a seasoned New Yorker, emerging from the subway in an unfamiliar section of town can be directionally daunting. Factor in emergencies, like if there's a subway fire and you need to grab a cab. Knowing the exact address to tell the driver is crucial because, believe me, he won't know Shetler Studios from shinola. If the audition is a typical Equity chorus call that adheres to all Equity procedures, plan to get to the studio one half hour before the audition. The sign-up sheet is read promptly at that time and cards handed out. After you write all of the directions down, pack your pen with the notes to be able to fill out the card with your name and general experience. For the truly industrious, make a trial run to visit the studio earlier in the week to get a feel for the surroundings and the studio facility itself.

Your picture, resume, and sheet music should be placed so they don't get crinkled. If your bag doesn't have a sturdy pocket, put them in a reinforced binder or sandwiched between two pieces of cardboard in a manila envelope. You may be asked to hand over your picture and resume in the studio itself, so place it where you can easily whip it out. How embarrassing it would be to unload your dirty tights, half-eaten bagel, and sweaty towel while you burrow to the bottom of your bag to find it.

There is no telling how long you will be at an audition so it is wise to pack a water bottle and something small to eat. Usually the male and female calls will be separated into morning and afternoon sessions so you know you won't be there more than four hours without a break, but I have been at calls that lasted from ten in the morning straight through until six-thirty at night. Actually on one such call there was a half-hour period where the casting people ate, but they didn't tell us. We stood around trying to keep warm, expecting to be called back onstage in a moment's notice. Nice, huh? Many studios have water fountains and vending machines, but if you are stuck in the audition room or onstage, you'll be thankful for your personal supply of water, fruit, crackers, or whatever else tides you over. Bringing a lot of money to a call is not a good idea since unfortunately there are people with sticky, stealing fingers, but small bills and loose change for a vending machine may offer just the relief you need.

An extra set of dance clothes could come in handy if you are asked to come back later in the day. Of course, this depends on how sweaty and smelly you normally get. If you can smell yourself, it's a guarantee others smell you threefold. An extra set of tights is a good idea for women just in case you get a horrific run or crotch tear. Warm clothes are a must. Studios can be roasting or freezing, both in summer and in winter. Many times the audition studio will heat up from crowds of dancers learning the combinations but when you hit the hallways you feel like you've stepped from a steam bath into the Finnish backwoods. If you are hot you can't do much with stripping down from your basic tights and leotards, but you can put on legwarmers and sweaters if you are chilly. Just be sure they are easy to put on or remove quickly.

Wearing your dance clothes under your street clothes to travel to an audition is a good idea until you are familiar with the various studios. Many have big dressing rooms, but some are minuscule. Even in the larger ones, if the call is a big one, you may find yourself nose to knees with someone else. Often you may have more than one call in a day. Throwing your street clothes on over your dance wear saves time, especially if the calls are tightly spaced. Wearing your dance clothes instead of carrying them also unburdens your dancebag. Toss in some undergarments if you finally want to peel out of your dance clothes at the end of the day.

When considering what street clothes to wear, know that you may be given time to change out of your dance wear before you go in to sing. This is a mental relief; it's a way of saying, "I won't have to dance again for them today." For the casting people, the singing portion is a golden opportunity to study your face, your body, and your natural stance. While casual is fine, you don't want to go in looking like a hobo. If there isn't time to change you may want to put on a shirt, sweater, jacket, or for females, a short skirt. Whereas I never thought twice about being in tights and a leotard in a dance call, I always felt a little naked singing. A miniskirt or silk jacket did the trick, doubling as a way to show off my legs. For those of you who don't know what to do with your hands while you sing, pants or a jacket with pockets can be a lifesaver.

The dance shoes you need depend on the type of call and the style of the choreographer. Some examples: Jerome Robbins always gave a simple ballet combination at the beginning of his auditions since he came from the ballet world. Therefore, you'd bring ballet shoes and character shoes or boots. The description of a show in a casting call may say that it is Busby Berkley in style and will star Gregory Hines. That's a no-brainer. You bring tap shoes, as well as character shoes and heels for women. I include character shoes because although the show may stress tap, there may be non-tap sections and you don't want to be slipping and sliding around the audition floor. Let's say there is a call for female dancers and it specifies strong pointe work. You would throw in your ballet shoes, pointe shoes, and heels in case they do differing sections from the show. Other calls may request nontraditional footwear like Rollerblades, Irish clogs, or sandals but these would always be mentioned in the breakdown. If you really don't know anything about a show, which is often the case for new shows, bring ballet shoes, character shoes or boots, jazz sneakers, and heels. Your bag may be a little heavy, but you will be prepared for any eventuality. Whatever shoes you bring, please check that the soles aren't about to tear or the heels ready to fall off. This happens far more often in auditions than you would imagine and every time it drives me nuts to watch these poor dancers slide and struggle along in stocking feet.

The toiletries you pack are up to your personal sense of hygiene and your hair style. Unless your hair is buzzed short, you'll need a comb or brush for a touch-up. Asking someone to borrow theirs is such a gross-out. If your hair relies on hair gel or hairspray to look halfway decent, pack them. A few tissues will get you through a runny nose, sweaty brow, or will let you wipe away any makeup that has melted into a raccoon pool below your eyes. You may not realize that physical exertion and flop sweat have made your pits less than rosy, so pack a deodorant. A toothbrush, toothpaste, or those cool little fingertip dental dots will remove any colorful food you might have eaten or will freshen your mouth if it feels cottony. For women, use a makeup bag that can hold basic makeup items like lipstick or gloss, powder, cheek color, and mascara, and that has room for feminine hygiene spray and tampons or pads. No one needs a steamer trunk to carry all of these items. Most drugstores have trial-size items on sale. They may not be your particular brand, but they will suffice to help comprise a lightweight kit. The advantage is, if you use this kit only for auditions, it will always be ready instead of you frantically emptying your medicine chest each time you have a call.

The last items you may want to toss in aren't essential, but may come in useful. Normally, if the dance combination involves floor work, the casting call will state to bring knee pads. But you never know. If the choreographer is known for athletic dancing, I'd throw them in. A book or portable cassette/CD player may help kill the time between auditions or if you are asked to come back later in the day. In case a leotard or bra strap rips, you'll be rescued if you have a couple of safety pins. A small towel serves a dual purpose of drying you off and keeping your neck warm when you drape it. When it is really hot and salty sweat plays havoc on your eyes, a bandana, either rolled or tied, will solve the problem. Last, pack something small that makes you simply feel darned good about yourself—a favorite saying, a photograph, a lucky penny. Whether you are feeling scared or invincible, these little objects can give you a moment's respite, a boost of confidence, and an inner smile.

Physical and Mental Preparation

The only time you have an inkling of what you'll be expected to do in an audition is for a replacement call. Usually the combination is something from the show. Otherwise, it's open season. Being ready physically, vocally, and spiritually will help you tackle whatever is thrown at you. After warming up vocally at home, I always took a dance class before any audition for two reasons. One, my muscles had a chance to wake up and work out the kinks. Two, dancing in my own world made me feel good about myself. It's rather like the freedom of performing the last preview before the critics come in. Many times no ballet or jazz class was offered early enough, so I would take an 8 A.M. stretch class. If there was absolutely no class, I'd give myself a barre at home. It was terribly important for me to rekindle the love I have for dance; this love never failed to carry over into the audition itself.

Other performers have their own preferences.

ROBERT MONTANO: I was practically always the first person at an audition. I arrived early to warm up and took time to get used to the surroundings so I wouldn't freak out with excitement. I waited for my competitors to come into my world as if it were my home—as if I invited you.

JoAnn M. Hunter: I hate auditioning so I am a last-second person. I warm up at home, maybe a little bit there, I get changed, get focused, go in, do my thing, have a good time, boom boom boom, and leave. I don't want anyone to think I'm a snob, but I'm not there to socialize. After it's over I'm like, "Let's play!" But in the meantime it's just horrible. People behind a desk staring at you, judging you. God! What could be worse?

Bebe Neuwirth: Part of me loved the social aspect of auditions since I had no social life growing up. You would warm up there and stretch and talk to the people around you. I enjoyed that.

Just as you do what is necessary to warm up your body, your singing muscles need a boost to ignite. The easiest, most systematic way is to vocalize along with one of your favorite voice lessons on your cassette while you shower or get dressed. Without the organized guidance of your tape, you may be tempted to stretch your chords too high too fast—sort of like splatting into a split as soon as you get out of bed. Once you are warm, sing your audition song a few times to be sure you remember the lyrics and to review any pointers your vocal coach has given you. But don't plague over it. Then as you travel to the studio, don't be ashamed to hum or sing. New York is a city of screwballs and professionals: the nuts talk out loud to their demons and the professionals rehearse. A great place to sing loudly is in the subway station as the express trains screech by. If you don't know what I mean, check out the train screaming scene in the film *Cabaret*.

The last thing you should allow time for is to calm your nerves, focus your mind, and be nice to yourself. Yoga helps some people; smiling at yourself in the mirror while slapping on cologne helps others. Whether this is your first New York audition or your fiftieth, take a moment to congratulate yourself for having the wherewithal to make it this far. You are talented, unique, and courageous.

Chita Rivera: When you need something too badly, you become frightened. Try not to let that fear take over. When a door in life opens, don't say, "I can't do this." Just look in. If you are curious, step in, unless it's something that is going to hurt you. It might open up a whole new world for you. That's what I did when others were afraid to go to an audition. I went, I danced right down in front. Once I got to do an imitation of Marilyn Monroe in a show when I'd never done an imitation before. It's so important to not let the desperation take over. Breathe. Have faith. If it's to be, it will be.

You are now ready to grab your dancebag and go.

CHAPTER TEN

Into the Jaws of the Beast:
The Audition

*To cast a show, Michael Bennett would always say to go with the talent.
Find people who do your work the best and use them and don't worry
about anything else. So in the chorus of* A Joyful Noise, *which was
Michael's first show, on one end of the line was Bayork Lee who was four
ten and a half, and on the other end of the line was Tommy Tune who was
six six and a half. It didn't matter to Michael. Added to that wisdom, my
philosophy is not to cast anybody in a show that I don't want to sit down
and have dinner with. I figure if I want to have dinner with them then
I've got a stage full of people who the audience is going to enjoy being with
for the evening.*

— Tommy Tune

When you walk into the hallway of the audition studio, your senses will
undoubtedly be assaulted. Sally Stretch will be polishing her earrings with
her kneecap, Peter Pirouette will be spinning in a two-by-two space and
bashing his knee into Alex Arrogant who will roll his eyes and snarl,
"Grow up," Carrie Catatonic will numbly go wherever a shoulder nudges
her, Danny and Donna Done-Three-Shows-Together will be dishing,
Tony Tap will be shuffling away even though it's not a tap call, Silent

Susie will be eying the contenders, Ilsa Intimidation will treat everyone as gnomes, Busy Barry will talk too loudly on his cell phone, poor Sammy Sullen will sit in the corner wondering how he is going to pay his rent, and all will be exuding nervous energy. Who cares? You sign in, get your number, fill out whatever card they hand you, and do whatever you personally need to do to get ready. If you have to go to the bathroom, close your ears to the rumors that bounce off the tiled walls of what the audition will entail and how many people they are looking for. If the choreographer comes into the bathroom, let her cut ahead of you in line. Then return to the hallway to wait for your group to be called.

JoANN M. HUNTER: Being five foot four and a mix racially, I would look at other women who were tall, blonde, and beautiful and I just thought, "How can I compete with these people?" Then I realized so much of getting a job is your own self-esteem. If you feel good about yourself, you show that confidence to other people. It is an appealing quality. Auditioning is a talent in itself. A mind-set. You can't let people psych you out.

MICHAEL KUBALA: I try to be confident in an audition, but you can't help but compare. I'll walk in and think, "Uh-oh. That person has great feet, look at that person's arms, this guy has great stretch, that one is more attractive than I am. I'm not going to get this job." We're not blind.

BEBE NEUWIRTH: Any time you don't give yourself permission or you question your right to be at an audition, you're sunk. It's not just permission, it's uber-permission, a necessity. You must believe you have the right to be there.

DAVID WARREN-GIBSON: I love to audition. I get to be anything I want to be in my own little world. I know I have to find a way inside of me to make them want me, to win them over. And I always did. When I was asked to audition for Bob Fosse I thought, "Sure. Why not?" I sang "Tomorrow" from *Annie*. A grown man singing a little girl's song! The theatre was a sea of blackness out there and I thought, "Gee, I have to fill all of that. I'd better be really loud." When I finished I doubled over laughing because I struck myself so funny. Bob walked up on the stage and goes, "Where are you from?" I said, "Well, I live here!" He said, "Do you want to move a little bit?" So I moved—over. He said, "No, no. Do you want to dance a little bit?" I said, "Sure!" We danced a bit and he finally said, "Do you want to do my show?" I said, "Okay." The show ended up being *Dancin'*. Now how cool is that?

While you wait in the hallway, there is an unspoken etiquette you should observe. Let's suppose there are so many people at an audition, they take you in groups of twenty and you are in the third group. When the first group exits the studio and the second enters to audition, don't ask anyone from the first to teach you the combination. You'll be resented. Some of the dancers may show their friends or go over the combination by themselves, but you are not allowed to join in. It's fine to watch to get a feel for the style, but don't try to pick up the exact steps and counts. The dancers may have learned it wrong or slathered on their own stylistic tendency.

LUIS PEREZ: Before the dance call there's really nothing you can do but warm up. You don't know what the combination is going to be. I see first group people teaching the combination, but I don't trust that. Too many people learn wrong. I'd rather walk in with a clean slate and learn the choreography the way I see it, not the way somebody else sees it.

On the other hand, after the first cuts when everyone has learned the combination, there is a new camaraderie between friends and strangers—like soldiers who have all faced the trenches together. No matter the reality of the competition, many dancers will join forces to review the combination in the hallways or studio before the next go-round. It's quite wonderful.

Your actual audition begins the moment you walk into the studio. Someone at the table will notice your height, weight, coloring, dress, and demeanor. That first impression will draw either a positive or negative intuitive response before you've executed one step. No matter the nerves, place your dancebag on the side and wait courteously for instructions. Be pleasant, friendly (but not chummy), and glad to be there. The director and choreographer are not only looking for talent, but also for people they would enjoy working with; people who will be receptive to the many demands and changes that happen when putting together a show. Treat the audition like a class, sans warm-up. You will have more fun and your abilities will shine. There are three undeniable facts to remember. One, it is absolutely true that the casting people want to like you. They need to hire people. Two, you will not do your best if nerves scatter your concentration. Three, nobody on either side of the table really knows anything. There's an inkling of the type they want and the standard of technique, but who will ultimately fit the bill remains to be seen.

CHITA RIVERA: The director and choreographer change their minds. They see someone with a sparkle and they go, "Oh, instead of having that character be a little tiny fat thing, it's perfect that she's . . ." whatever. Everybody is different and everybody has something to offer. You may be the very jewel in the crown. You are that special.

All choreographers and casting directors have their own methods of conducting auditions. Usually an initial cut is necessary because there is no time to teach everyone all the different combinations. As disappointing as it is that you may get cut, they are actually doing you a favor. There is no sense wasting your entire day when they know from the git-go if they want you, and you may miss another audition that is perfect for you. The two types of initial cuts are nondance typecasting, and cutting down by giving a simple step or a short combination. The next processes are to give varying combinations to the smaller group(s), cut from there, request this smaller group to sing, and finally to grant an even smaller group a callback where all prospects from both the invited calls and the chorus calls are lumped together.

Nondance Typecasting

BEBE NEUWIRTH: If you could type me out, thank you. Then I know that it was nothing that I did—that "Jeez, maybe I didn't dance well enough or I didn't sing well enough" kind of feeling. I'm not blonde. I'm only five foot four. If I'm not right for it? Fine, type me out. It saves a lot of time and anxiety.

JOANN M. HUNTER: How can you just type somebody? They don't talk to you, see anything of your talent. The least they can do is watch you dance for a few minutes. You've worked so hard just to get there—you study every day, you're broke, you get up, put on your makeup, warm up, and all they do is line you up by twenty and go, "You stay, you stay," and half the time it's because someone knows you. I know. I've been on the other side of the table saying, "Keep him. He's a good egg." I think it's horrible.

It's important to remember the number you have been assigned because you will be called in by groups of ten to twenty, not by name. You will walk in with confidence, line up across the room, and literally get looked at, talked about in whispers, and judged for your physical attributes. Those few minutes may feel like a century. Every flaw, real or imagined, may magnify itself in your mind. You are not sure whether to catch their eyes or not, whether to smile or not, and whether to stand posed or be coolly, falsely relaxed. Being a dancer whose craft is movement, I always found the standing still torturous. The first time I had to go through typecasting was in front of Graciela Daniele for the Milliken Breakfast Show, a huge industrial in New York that hired the crème de la crème of Broadway. All of a sudden the nerves that I was trying to keep hidden congregated at my knees and they started jerking up and down faster than a sewing machine. When I looked down, my entire skirt was rippling out of control for all the world to see. I was mortified, but at least I was kept and ultimately got the job.

Out of each group certain lucky people will be asked to wait in the hall until all the typing is done. You may be pointed to, your number called, or your card taken from you. Everyone else will be dismissed with "Others, thank you for coming," spoken by the stage manager or casting director. If you get cut, courteously pick up your dancebag, exit the room, and leave the studio facility as soon as possible for your own peace of mind, unless there is another audition you are planning to attend.

Typing Out With a Simple Step or Short Combination

Many choreographers want to see the dancers move but don't want to spend a lot of time teaching a combination. It may be as simple as traveling across the floor one to three at a time, in numeric sequence, doing a waltz clog, as I had to do in the open call for *Hello, Dolly!* Often it is a common ballet move like chassé-pas-de-bourée-glissade-assemblé, prep second, fourth, double pirouette, land fourth. Whatever the combination, it will be movement that is familiar to a classroom. This little time-saving procedure shows an immense amount of information about the dancer. If the dancer has trouble with the basic steps or is nearly rigid with exertion, it is a high sign that he is a beginner. If the dancer performs the combination dourly, it raises a red flag that while she may be technically proficient, her performance quality may be boring. If the dancer executes the steps but mugs and smiles excessively, it rings of an amateur. Finally if the dancer breezes through the combination with such confidence, joy, and ease that it looks as second nature as a dolphin in water, it is a surety that the choreographer will want to investigate the dancer further.

Have no fear if the combination is pure ballet. The main objective is to see how the musical theatre dancer handles basic ballet steps. After all, an assemblé is an assemblé, and port de bras is port de bras whether you are in ballet slippers or jazz shoes. Likewise, if you are from a strong ballet background but the combination is funky, don't panic. Use the technique you have to figure out the moves, and let the choreographer be the judge.

The choreographer may give the first section of a longer combination. Within the steps will be one of the styles in the show and the typical technique the choreographer tends to employ. You will be on unfamiliar ground in this case since each show is unique. Try to pick up not only the steps, but also the intent. At this primary stage of typing, flubbing a step may not be as important as your overall technique, style, and demeanor.

Sometimes the basic combination is a set ritual, as Bob Fosse used to do with his "Tea For Two" combination, Michael Bennett with his "State your name, age, where you're from, and then do a time step and a classical double pirouette" for *A Chorus Line*, or it may be a specific section of an existing show.

ROBERT MONTANO: At an audition for *A Chorus Line* I was so nervous I said, "Hi. My name is Robert Montano and I'm a studio at Adelphi University. I take that back. I mean I'm a student!" What a moron.

If you know that the audition will always begin with the same combination, by all means learn it ahead of time from a friend if you can. If the show is running, see the show to at least get the style of the movement. If a dance class is offered that teaches combinations from shows, fork up the money to take it. It may not be exactly what is given in the audition so you'll need to listen up, but having 90 percent of the information is better than none at all. The truth is that you are not out to fool anybody by knowing the combination ahead of time. The extent of your technique at any particular time is what it is, and simply knowing you have to do the neat double pirouette is not going to make it miraculously happen. But you will be able to practice insecure moves and in the meantime become a better dancer.

As in the case of nondance typecasting, those selected will be asked to stay to learn another combination and the others will be dismissed. In some cases, this will be done by reading off the numbers and in others they will call out the names. Pay attention! There is no guarantee that the names and numbers will be in order so wait until you hear, "All others, thank you very much." If you are thanked, hide your disappointment, gather your belongings, and leave the studio without dawdling. Resist the temptation to ask if your number was called. Without fail at every audition I have ever given, someone has come up to me and asked if they were called to stay. Having to say, "No," is terribly awkward for both parties. If another dancer sneezed in your ear during the cut, you may ask the stage manager or casting director if they will recheck, but don't expect too much.

GRACIELA DANIELE: Cutting down, it really depends on the demands of the show and how many people I am hiring. In big shows I try to cut down with a short combination so I don't spend three days in preliminaries. For a show that doesn't have too many people I like not to cut until the second combination since the first that I do is usually balletic, while the second has stylistically the demands of the show. There are some cases in which the ballet technique is not very good, but I can see in the dancer something that is very interesting to explore.

Varying Combinations

Congratulations! You have made the first cut. Most likely you will be asked for your picture and resume at this point so that the casting people can read more about you and begin to match your name and face with your experience. If they are planning a series of cuts, they may not ask for the picture and resume until you sing.

Now the real work begins. There is no foreseeing how many combinations you will be asked to learn or how quickly. Perhaps it will be a continuation of the section given for the first cut, or it may be totally new. The length and number of combinations depend on how many styles are within the show, if they are looking for more technically advanced people to be featured, and the time constraint of how long the studio is rented. The best thing is to pick up the steps as quickly and accurately as possible.

Where you stand to learn the combination is entirely up to you—where you feel most comfortable.

LUIS PEREZ: I thought people placed you in an audition, or at least there'd be the discipline and courtesy as in a ballet company. But in my first Broadway audition they called everyone out and, whoosh, the herd surged forward. I'm like, "Whoa! What is this? A zoo?" From then on I knew I wasn't one of those front line people. I'd walk into the room and stand in the back where I had room, knowing I could pick up really quickly. Then as they'd rotate lines, when I'd come up front, I'd show that I knew it.

BEBE NEUWIRTH: I always tried to get myself where I could see the combination clearly. I didn't shy away or stay back, nor did I push, but I was close to the front. Everyone needs to find what works for them.

Some misinformed dancers think that verbal or physical intimidation is the way to gain the edge. If anyone utters a demeaning comment to you, pay no attention. Your energy needs to fuel your positive attitude, not their evil insecurity. If a kicker or pusher targets you while you are learning a combination, move to a different part of the room. At one audition an idiot latched onto me like she had a vendetta against me. She accidentally-on-purpose kicked me repeatedly while we danced, and followed me wherever I moved. I found my attention gravitating more toward her than the combination so I calculated a timely, swift port de bras to her stomach, knocked the wind out of her, and as she wheezed I whispered, "Next time I'll tear your heart out." It made me sick to my stomach to resort to such tactics, but she left me alone. If you are forced into an unwitting battle, choose your tactics carefully and always try civility first. Most times an "Excuse me, do you realize you are hitting me?" is all it takes.

<u>ROBERT MONTANO</u>: I noticed that at an audition I was slowly being pushed to the back of the room, and the guys who were booking these gigs were up front, staying up front, and wearing black! So I made a decision to do the same—get close to the front without stepping on anyone's toes, and be seen. Because if you don't get seen, you don't get the job.

Since the theatre is such a small world, undoubtedly some dancers will be on a first-name basis with the choreographer or the assistant. Don't let this intimidate you. Not all dancers are right for particular shows, no matter the history. You may not see these people getting cut, but that's no guarantee they will get the show.

Often the assistant choreographer or the dance captain will demonstrate the combinations while the choreographer looks on. A good assistant will be specific with the moves and counts, change lines often to give everyone an equal chance, divide the dancers into two or three medium-sized groups to practice having more space, and demonstrate the combination with you until you can be weaned off their help. Within this time the choreographer often makes adjustments in the steps, provides acting intent, and stresses dynamics or rhythms. In worst cases, the counts will be replaced by sounds or even silence, as if everyone intuitively hears the accompaniment. Translate the moves into counts or phrases as best you can until you later hear the music and can try to marry the movement to it. An even harder scenario is when the choreographer is making up the combination off the top of his head. He may do something once, then turn and say, "What did I do?" When faced with this predicament, I would let the eager beavers hash out a comprehensive version unless I was smack dab behind him. In that case, I'd do my best to repeat a semblance of the move to show I could pick up quickly. After all, if choreographing on the spot was his modus operandi in an audition, it's a guarantee that is how he would conduct rehearsals.

While you are learning the combination avoid the temptation to ask too many questions. Many people make the mistake of thinking that asking questions will draw attention to them. Well, actually, they are right. But it is the wrong kind of attention. The choreographer will recognize it as a warning sign that the questioner is not listening and observing, doesn't have enough technique to figure it out, or is simply a time-wasting pain in the butt. Pick up as much of the combination as you can, and if there is a trouble spot, bide your time. Watch carefully each time that particular section is demonstrated. Tune in to the other dancers when they perform the steps in smaller groups and see if anyone else is having trouble with the same spot. Nine times out of ten, the choreographer will notice the glitch if it is widespread and will offer a more detailed explanation to the whole room. If you are still in the dark when it nears the time to perform, then feel free to ask for help.

Once the group has the choreography basically in hand, you will perform in groups of three or four, one or two times. This is when you will be judged. The choreographer will already have a basic idea of your talent from observing the larger groups, but the group of three is the time to gather your wits and wow them. Your performance, your acting, should match the style and mood of the combination. If it is a celebratory cakewalk, show that you enjoy the movement with a bright, energetic countenance. The energy may erupt into a smile, but don't force it. A tense, plastered smile is unnatural. If the combination is slow, sensuous, or serious, obviously you don't want to grin like a clown. Let the language and intent of the movement translate onto your face. (One trick to make a smile work is not to keep your head front, grinning and staring blankly, like you are selling to the audience, but to let your head flow naturally with the épaulement.)

Once the groups of three have performed, a cut may happen, another combination may be taught, or you may be asked to sing. Go with the flow with renewed vigor. The competition is now both narrowed down and formidable, but as long as you are still there, you've got a shot at the prize.

At this point of the audition, let me offer you another piece of unspoken etiquette. After this longer portion of the audition, the choreographer may need to take a bathroom break. If you have been cut, don't approach them unless it is to say that the audition was the most fun you've had in years, and if you are kept, don't ask any questions about the audition or the show. This is a tough thing for a young dancer. You'd like to know why you were cut or what to work on to improve your dancing. It's not the choreographer's job to give explanations. If you have stood out in their minds, they may offer a suggestion or an explanation on their own discretion. At one audition I absolutely adored a tall, red-headed young man. His eagerness was invigorating and infectious, his manners impeccable, and his technique solid. But he was simply too young for the show. It broke my heart to cut him so I sought him out in the hallway to explain. Discouragement literally lifted off his shoulders as I spoke with him when he realized he wasn't cut for his talent.

GRACIELA DANIELE: My first audition in New York was for a summer stock tour of *West Side Story*. I had never been in a theatre audition in my life because I was from the ballet world. We did combination after combination, I was kept, and then we did the singing part. I sang a little bit in English—badly, since I didn't speak English—and a little bit in French. Finally there were maybe three girls left. The choreographer called me aside and said that I was an exceptional dancer, but I didn't have a Latin look. I went, "Qué?" According to the American idea I don't look Latin because I'm Argentinean—more European looking— than darker Puerto Rican. I thought, "This is a strange system. I have the talent to do the work, but they won't take me because I'm not Latin enough." I could barely speak English I was so Latin! But I appreciated his taking the time to explain.

Singing Audition

The group that is asked to sing will wait in the hall until they are called in one by one. As I mentioned in the previous chapter, you may or may not be given a chance to change clothes. The stage manager or casting director may ask if anyone needs to go first because of a commitment like a rehearsal or matinee so you may sing out of order. While you won't know the full lineup, you will be told when you are the next one in. Use the waiting time to drink some water, go over your lyrics, and gently but not obnoxiously warm up.

Carry your sheet music in hand when you enter the studio. It's okay to cheerfully say hello to the table, as long as you don't sound like a mouse before a feline guillotine. It is not necessary to say your name. Hand your picture and resume to the stage manager then go immediately to the piano. Briefly explain the format of your sheet music to the audition pianist, the tempo you would like, and point out any tricky places. Be courteous and friendly to the pianist. Not only will your attitude be noted by the table, but many a famous composer started as a rehearsal or audition pianist. One well-known Broadway composer I know remembers everyone who was nasty to him during auditions years ago and will not hire them to this day.

Next, go to the center of the room to sing. Sometimes you will be asked a form of "What do you have for us?" If so, say the name of the song and the show it is from. Often the auditioner offers the information before beginning to sing. Is it a good practice? I'm not convinced. It certainly isn't necessary and on one occasion the musical director whispered angrily to me, "What does he think I am? Stupid? Like I won't recognize the song?" If you have a large repertoire, don't ask, "What would you like to hear?" Ultimately the answer will be, "What have you got?" and the next few minutes will be wasted deciding who wants to hear which favorite song. Pick a comfortable song to sing and if the musical director wants to hear more, she'll ask.

EUGENE FLEMING: At my audition for *A Chorus Line*, the musical director asked me to sing part of Richie's song. I said, "I can't sing that high!" He said it eight times and every time I was like, "You've got to be kidding. It's too high." Then T. Michael Reed, who was holding the audition, yelled, "Sing it!" I was so scared, those high notes came flying out. He was like, "See?" So that was that. I was offered the role.

A question that plagues many a dancer is where to look when you sing. If you are auditioning in a theatre, you're golden. You can sing out to the orchestra or mezzanine comfortably since the casting people aren't right on top of you. In a studio my suggestion is to focus directly over the casting people's heads, occasionally shifting to the corners or catching their eye as the lyrics to your song dictate. Staring at the people is unwise. One guy I auditioned must have read somewhere to pick a person out at the table and sing to them. Unfortunately, the person was me. He sang some love song that made me squirm because it felt too intimate. Throughout the song he slowly inched toward me and by the end he was at the edge of the table cooing into my face. What was I supposed to do? React back? All I know is I didn't register a note and when he left the room the other casting people roared with laughter not at him, but at me. He was forgotten. On the other hand, a comic song can be effective singing directly to the casting people, as long as you include all of them. The goal is to tell the story of the song, and to let the lyrics guide the focus.

When you have finished your song, retrieve your sheet music and your dancebag and leave with confidence. If they have any questions for you, they will ask. Otherwise, they are waiting for you to get out of there so that they can discuss your possibilities, get on with the next person, or simply to take a moment to stretch their legs. Unless they are extremely desperate for a replacement in a show, they will not offer you a job at that time. If you are lucky you will receive a phone call for a callback in the next few days or weeks. Don't give up hope until you hear on the street that the callbacks are actually taking place. Some auditions are so large-scale, the callbacks don't come for quite some time.

Callbacks

While you anxiously check your answering machine fifty times a day to hear if you get a callback, review the dance combinations you were given. Most likely, you will have to perform them again. Rehearse any trouble spots you may have had with your song, and go over your second song in case they want to hear something else. You won't be wasting your time because even if you don't get called, you'll be further along with your song for the next audition. If you receive a callback, pat yourself on the back and prepare your dancebag and yourself as you did for the initial call. It's a good idea to wear the same outfit as before. Obviously they liked you in that style and repeating what you first showed them sparks their memory. Although the casting director should have your picture and resume, pack another one just in case yours was misplaced. Don't take it personally—everyone is human.

There won't be as many people at the callback, but you will see new faces that were chosen from the invited calls. Also, the women and men may now be together so that the casting people can mix and match looks. The procedure will be pretty much the same as the first call, though combinations that were previously taught will only be reviewed, not explained from the giddy-up. It is highly likely you will be taught yet another combination to further investigate your talent and style. During the callback, usually after singing, you may be asked if you have any conflicts with the projected rehearsal and performance schedule of the show. Speak up if you truly have a problem. It is inconsiderate and unprofessional to spill the bad news later when they have assumed you are free and eager to do the show.

After you dance and sing, some people may be handed sides to read for one-liners, small roles, or for understudy considerations. If you are not asked to read, don't fret. You may be perfect for the ensemble but not for the few lines that need to be given out. (Many times these lines won't be assigned until rehearsal when the director has more time to get to know you.) If you are asked to read, normally you are given a brief breakdown of who the character is or what the situation happens to be. Use your common sense to glean the characterization from the script and speak without affectation. Chances are, with this type of cold reading, they just want to see if you can handle talking out loud. If you are truly being considered for a role, you will be given complete sides and ample time to work on them until your second callback. (Actors' Equity allows only two callbacks. Some people take advantage of this; some don't find it necessary.)

As in the first audition, you won't be offered a job on the spot but must wait for the official phone call. When you receive it, whoop, holler, laugh, cry, whatever—offering a job is one phone call casting directors don't mind making. Then listen up. You will be told what type of contract is being offered, when and where it is to be signed, and whether or not a six-month rider is attached. The casting director may tell you the schedule or may say that the production stage manager will be in touch soon. Unless you have an agent, the pay will probably be minimum Broadway scale. If more experienced dancers have their agents bargain for more money, so what? This is your first show. If enough agents bargain for more money, the producers may decide to offer a favored nations contract for the ensemble where everyone gets the same above-scale pay. You will be included in this arrangement, agent or no.

EUGENE FLEMING: The day I joined *A Chorus Line* I landed on payday. I called my dad and said, "Dad, they paid me. They gave me six hundred bucks and I ain't done nothing yet!" He said, "Hey, that dancing's all right, man!" Damn, that was great.

One occurrence may happen that can rock you. Every show needs a male and female swing. Swings do not have their own part, but must learn everyone else's part of the same gender in case anyone is out of the show. It's a hard job, and you may be disappointed that you don't get your own track, but if you think you can handle it, take the job. You will not only be in the cast of a Broadway show, but you will work very closely with the dance captain. A good swing is extremely valuable to the production and down the line you may take over an onstage slot or request a slot when the show goes out on the national tour.

J IM BORSTELMANN: I was one of the "Steam Heat" dancers in *Pajama Game* at City Opera. Jerry Robbins' assistant saw me and asked me to audition for *Jerome Robbins' Broadway* because they needed swings. I got the job—my first Broadway show! I loved being a swing. I could be a Jet and a Shark, do the bottle dance in "Tradition," and be the bottom half of Fruma-Sarah. Honey, that was great. Wow! Did I take her around! The number with the doors? I did all the different roles. I came to the theatre excited every day, thinking, "What am I going to get to do today?" I would have hated doing just one track.

If you do not get an offer, know that simply by making it to the callback you were singled out of the crowd for your talent. Your picture and resume will stay on file for replacements, a future request to audition, or the choreographer may add you to his personal file for a different show. What you are wrong for today, you may be right for tomorrow.

M AMIE DUNCAN-GIBBS: I didn't get everything I auditioned for, but it's a good thing. I learned how to deal with rejection, realizing it's not personal. Some people are going to like me and some are going to think I have no talent. I went to one Broadway audition just after having my first child. They were so rude. "You're terrible," this and that. The next day I had a call for a different Broadway show and almost didn't go. But I got that job. Within twenty-four hours I was told I was horrible and then told I was great.

I sincerely hope that one day you receive the thrilling phone call that tells you that you have landed a Broadway show. After years of hard work, it is the fulfillment of your dream. In the next chapter I describe what your new job entails and offer advice on how to relive your dream time after time, show after show, until one day you wake up and marvel, "Holy cow! I've built a career."

CHAPTER ELEVEN

Working on the Great White Way

When you get a Broadway show you become a member of a new family, and what an exhilarating family it is! On the morning of the first rehearsal the creative juices from all departments eddy throughout the studio on a wave of excitement. As the newest member of the family, you get to drink this heady beverage, knowing that your talent adds to its potency. Faces may look familiar or foreign. If you know no one, don't worry; it won't be for long. Soon you will be acquainted with your great-grandparents (the producers), your grandparents (the author, composer, and lyricist), your parents (the director, choreographer, and musical director), your aunts and uncles (the design team), your surrogate parents (the stage management), and your brothers and sisters (the cast). Cousins will eventually abound in the form of rehearsal pianists, hairstylists, makeup artists, dressers, the tech crew, musicians, company managers, and all the assistants from the various departments. This is not a family reunion where old joys and pains are rehashed. You are enveloped in a new family whose common goal is to create a spectacular baby—a Broadway show.

Each show takes its own route to Broadway. Some start in workshops or regional theatres, some go out of town for tryouts and then come immediately into New York, and some play out of town, close down, and resume months later. If the workshop has already happened, the show may rehearse in New York and move directly to the theatre. The whys and wherefores run the gamut from finances to theatre availability and are too suppositious to list. However, for the performers, the basics are the basics no matter where you are.

Rehearsals

On the first rehearsal day for the first hour or so, an Equity representative ensures that contracts are signed and explains union rules and procedures. The cast fills out numerous insurance cards, elects an Equity deputy, and may vote on whether to take an hour lunch as opposed to an hour and a half. If you have any questions about the various forms, feel free to ask the representative. As far as paying dues and initiation fees, arrangements can be made to deduct a certain amount each week from your paycheck so you don't have to fork over too much money at once. After the Equity business is finished, there is normally a read-through of the script, including songs, so that everyone understands what the show is about. Many times the set designer shows a model of the set. Normally you stay in your street clothes for the business section of the morning and the read-through. However, depending on the schedule, you may dive right into dancing as soon as the read-through and lunch are over so be sure to have your dance clothes with you.

The tools you need each day for rehearsal are your dance clothes, appropriate shoes, a battery-operated cassette recorder, and blank tapes to record your musical rehearsals. Some performers, especially women, bring different styles of shoes so their feet don't ache from being in heels all day. Personally, I find that wearing heels to learn the choreography is wise if that is indeed the type of shoe you will wear in the show. The choreographer will experiment with certain moves and lifts that could be drastically altered in a different type of shoe. But, once you sit down to learn music or read a scene, slip off the heels to give yourself a break if you are uncomfortable.

Your main job in the rehearsal process is to learn the choreography, staging, and music as quickly as possible. The time constraints in mounting a production are enormous. When you are not being used, review the material you have been given. Each evening memorize your lyrics and harmonies at home, and commit the choreography to both mental and muscle memory. Plunging ahead is usually the name of the rehearsal game, so you may not touch the material you have been taught for another week or two. No one expects perfection, but if you have forgotten everything you are dead meat. Professionals in the ensemble are not led by the nose and granted private coaching because of laziness. Taking your job seriously will be the foundation of building your reputation and your career.

Prior to or during the rehearsal weeks costume fittings are scheduled, starting with taking your measurements and ending with putting the finishing touches on the final product. It is a marvel to observe how the costume designer painstakingly works to capture the style of the show, including the color palette of the entire production, with the set and lighting designers. Therefore, it is not your business to comment on color or cut at your fittings, especially as a newcomer. You have not yet earned that right, and many times what may look weird in the mirror looks wonderful onstage. However, it is your responsibility to make sure you can move in the costume. The choreographer cannot describe every single step to the designer, so if you find yourself performing a cartwheel in one number or a knee slide in another, relay the information at your earliest fitting. If the number has not yet been choreographed, there are particular stress points on the costume to test. Can you kick over your head, do a grand plié in second, and a full lunge? Can you move your arms in every extreme direction? Can you bend fully forward and fully back? The time to add gussets, slits, or reinforcements is in the fitting, not in the final dress rehearsal, so courteously speak up. The designer may get frustrated at the moment, but in the end, you save the destruction of a very expensive costume during the run of the show. If the costume seems to be completely unworkable, explain the situation to the choreographer and adjustments in the dance or design area will be discussed.

The closer you get to moving to the theatre for tech rehearsals, the more the tension builds. There is a race to finish staging the show, daily changes in the script are handed out, and run-throughs are performed for the designers, producers, and advisors. New songs, requiring new choreography, may be inserted; publicity sessions may steal precious rehearsal time; and a sense of success or failure may leak into the rumor mill. Once you move to the theatre, all of this activity seems to grind to a halt as each moment of the show is analyzed for the proper lighting, set moves, and costume changes. Your day stretches into "ten out of twelves," meaning you will work a five-hour period starting at midday, have a two-hour break, then work another five. As tired as you may be after days of this schedule, remember that the director, choreographer, designers, stage management, and tech crew often start their day at 8 A.M. and stay for note sessions until way past midnight. The wisest thing you can do is to take care of yourself as best as possible without petty complaint. If you have to run the hardest number in the show at 11:30 P.M. after standing on your feet all day, so be it. You are a slave to the schedule.

Many seasoned performers go to the theatre to claim their places in the dressing rooms the evening before the first theatre rehearsal or early on the exact day. The stage management will have assigned which room you will be in, but within that room it's technically first come, first serve. For a newcomer, you must remember that as much as you have become a part of the family, there is an unwritten hierarchy of respect and the more prime spaces should go to the more experienced people. Sometimes name tags are taped to the mirrors, but unless the assignment is for costume considerations, they are interchangeable. Admittedly, I have been known to rearrange the tags after I had a few shows under my belt with no one being the wiser. Each dressing room is different so you have to take into consideration the placement of sinks, toilets, doors, costume racks, vents, shelves, and walking paths. That is all I will tell you. This trade secret is one I feel you should learn on your own. Whatever your space turns out to be, you must keep your belongings within that space. Feel free to decorate it as you wish, although there is a superstition that you don't go all out until after opening. If the show is a hit you will own the space for a while. If not, like a migrant, you may have to quickly move out.

At some point in the transition from studio to theatre you will experience a day of respite and delight—the sitz probe. This is when you hear the full orchestrations for the first time in a music studio. Number by number the cast listens and sings with the orchestra while the conductor gives brief corrections. After weeks of rehearsing to piano, you finally hear what the composer has envisioned in his head all along. It is thrilling, often surprising, sometimes puzzling, but never disappointing. From that moment on you are spoiled by its splendiferousness.

Previews

When you first get into previews, the public performances before the opening, your hours are still "ten out of twelve," rehearsing in the afternoon and performing at night. (According to Equity rules and depending on the running length of the show, there is usually not a rehearsal on two-show days.) Script, music, and choreographic changes fly at you left and right, all of which have to be teched again and translated to all departments. The difficulties at this stage of the game are performing these changes in front of an audience and closing your ears to the theatre gossip of whether you have a hit or a flop. The whole idea behind previews is to test the show without judgment until opening night, but unfortunately, many people like to be soothsayers and critics. Focus into your job, enjoy your performance, and let the problems plague the higher-ups.

A particularly unpleasant scenario is if the director, choreographer, or musical director is fired or a show doctor comes in to make improvements. Warranted or not, this is a trying time within the family, like a nasty divorce. No matter your loyalties, there is ultimately nothing you can do about it. Keeping a positive attitude and welcoming the stepparent with respect will be appreciated by all.

There will definitely be a hair designer for the show and perhaps a makeup designer if the show is in a distinct period. If a wig has been designed for you, whatever you do with your natural hair is up to you because it will be covered. However, if you use your own hair, you must adhere to the design and color dictated by the designer. As a matter of fact, a "hair clause" is usually in your contract stating that you agree to do whatever is asked, within reasonable limits. Upkeep is provided in the theatre by the hairstylists. The makeup artist teaches you how to design your face, but applying the makeup each night eventually becomes your responsibility.

TOMMY TUNE: The art of makeup has always fascinated me. The first time I saw American Ballet Theatre, I went backstage after the performance and was shocked at what the dancers looked like. Their faces were covered in orange greasepaint and their eyes and lips were painted on. When I first came to Broadway they would teach the guys a makeup style and we were required to learn it and put it on. Back then the lighting was harsher so it would wipe away everything. We'd have to paint our features on so we wouldn't be faceless wonders out there. Nowadays guys don't wear makeup as much, I think because the lighting has become more sophisticated. You don't have to make your face travel as much; the lights do it.

MAMIE DUNCAN-GIBBS: You know how some people are cute and they get things because they're cute? I was never cute. I always had to study for the test. People didn't just smile at me and give me a B. That's what I love about theatre. No matter how I feel, I can walk into the theatre and by the time I put on the wig and makeup, I'm ready to go. It's the magic of theatre.

The Run of the Show

The day after the opening the cast grins or grumbles over the reviews while the producers weigh the prospects of the show and organize publicity campaigns. The director and choreographer may show up at the theatre, but usually they take a well-deserved vacation. Of course you will see them again, but they are no longer a daily presence. Your new parents are the stage management and dance captain who will maintain the cleanliness of the show, conduct rehearsals, and solve myriad problems. Treat them with the respect they deserve and take their notes without long-winded explanations or complaint. They are doing double duty overseeing the show while performing or calling it themselves. I acted as dance captain on many shows and inwardly groaned at those I had to nursemaid or who were hostile to notes.

As you settle into the eight-shows-a-week schedule, it is a given as a professional that you perform your show each matinee and evening as if you were doing it for the first time. The audience pays dearly to see you and it is your responsibility to deliver the goods. You must be punctual, dependable, remain consistent with the choreography and direction, and approach rehearsals with energy. What is not a given is your backstage behavior. In a word, courtesy.

LUIS PEREZ: Everybody in the theatre is working toward the same thing whether it's the guy who's setting up the props or the guy who's filling the water bottles. It's important to respect everyone and their jobs because people are people and people remember the way you treat them. You never know who is going to end up where. Which dresser is going to be the next major costume designer or head of wardrobe? Which assistant director is going to be the next hotshot director, or rehearsal pianist the next Broadway composer? Is the person next to you in the ensemble going to be the next Rob Marshall? If you are a mean son of a bitch or a nasty person, you'd better look around and hand out some respect or else your career will backfire.

Courtesy boils down to manners and a mind-set. For example, while it is true that the dressers fall into the servile category, they should not be considered your maids or whipping boys. Simply caring for your costumes, picking up after yourself, and saying, "Thank you," gains friendship and respect from these union professionals. Making small talk with the stage crew and musicians guarantees a warm welcome, performance after performance, production after production. Each smile, each act of kindness, ensconces you into the entire theatrical community and believe me, the community will reciprocate the respect and care back to you, perks included.

JoAnn M. Hunter: If you get one show, you think it's a fluke. The second, okay, I might be on to something here. I think your reputation has a lot to do with it. I'm a hard worker, fairly easy to get along with. I don't talk back. I'm not trouble. I speak up for myself, but I do what I'm told unless it doesn't feel right. Like anything in life, how you act is so important, not just your talent. As a dance captain I've held a lot of auditions. Let's say you're holding a replacement call and you're down to two people. They're both good dancers. One is great to get along with, has great energy and stability. You know you can count on him. The other is a pain in the ass. Who do you think gets hired?

While you are not performing in the theatre, there are a number of things you can do to keep your daylight hours fruitful and interesting. Of utmost importance is to keep your audition skills up. It is so easy to relax into your current job, forgetting that you inevitably will have to audition again. Taking a daily dance class expands your technique, especially if the show is not physically demanding. It also helps alleviate aches and pains due to the stress of performing the same movements night after night. A dance class, particularly one in a different style from the show, stretches and strengthens the affected areas of the body.

Though you may not want to audition for another Broadway show right away, you can develop your performing abilities and pump up your resume by auditioning for television and film, workshops, nightclub acts, and choreographers' auditions. These rehearsals and performances are mostly geared around the Broadway schedule and offer vast opportunities to work with new people on new projects. While it is a bit exhausting to double up, your creativity will be energized, both in the new project and in your current show. It just might happen that the workshop you do this year goes into production next year when your show is closing. Other rewarding opportunities to perform are in the many benefits, like the Easter Bonnet Competition, that take place throughout the year. Your status as a Broadway performer will be appreciated and welcomed.

If you are so inclined, now is the time to investigate an agent. Some dancers don't feel they need one and would rather not pay commissions. Many dancers find work on their own, either by going to the chorus calls or by being specifically requested by a choreographer. This way certainly works as long as you keep yourself up to date on what shows are in the planning stages. However, the advantage of having an agent is that casting directors inform the agent of all auditions, some of which may be private calls and not posted by Equity. For shows that do have an Equity chorus call, the agent submits your name to casting directors to secure an appointment for an invited call rather than having to deal with the multitudes. When it comes time for negotiation, your agent bargains for you and informs you of any fine print on the contract that you may not understand. This buffer between you and the general management can make your personal relationship with the producers far more congenial.

LUIS PEREZ: My first agent, Mary Day, contacted me while I was in the Joffrey and I booked a lot of commercials. But when I landed *West Side Story* it was the first time I had to deal with a Broadway-type contract. She called and said, "Okay, this is how much you're getting paid. Now we have to talk about billing." I had no idea what she was talking about so I said, "Billing? Well, you can bill me once a month for your commission if you want. Or I'll pay you weekly." She said, "No, I was able to get you billing above Riff on the show poster," so I said, "Oh, is that important?"

Ideally, a good agent will invest their time into building your future, and not just sit back and collect the commission on your current show. Many agencies have television, film, and commercial departments so together, you and your agent can broaden your career. It can be a very rewarding partnership.

ROBERT MONTANO: It's like a marriage. You've got to be able to speak to your agent and vice versa. Where I come from, loyalty is huge. And it's rare to find that in this business—rare. However, if you have faith, just know they're out there. My current agent, Steve Stone, is rare and simply the best. He's smart, young, creates allies, and, above all, he's loyal.

My personal opinion is that a dancer doesn't need an agent as a new-comer. Once you land a show or two, your name and worth are more spotlighted. You can then ask an agency if they would negotiate your next contract for you on an independent basis. Technically, you have gotten the job yourself and you are paying them to do the paperwork, but a relationship can bud without the obligations of being signed. When you are in a show, I suggest you provide tickets to willing theatrical and commercial agents to come and see you and discuss if they would like to represent you. Once you feel comfortable with a particular person, you can sign a longer-term agreement. If you do decide to work with an agent, remember that he is representing you and is responsible for getting your name out there, but only you and your talent can get you the job.

BEBE NEUWIRTH: When I came to Broadway with *A Chorus Line* I was understudying Sheila. I knew I was going to be on for three weeks so I sent out a mailing to a lot of agents and offered to buy them tickets to see me. I think only one person came out of all that and I worked with him for a while.

A Broadway gig allows you to both spend and save money wisely. New head shots, voice lessons, and acting classes are now affordable without struggle. Your Actors' Equity medical insurance covers doctors, dental checkups, eye examinations, and limited chiropractic and massage therapy, which can be a great burden off your wallet. If the show runs, you may be able to afford your own apartment or at least cut down on room-mates. Finally, after years of denial, you can go to a restaurant after the show, buy a new outfit, or spend money on a loved one without sweat-ing the bill.

CHITA RIVERA: On my first Broadway show I earned two hundred and fifty dollars. Whoa! That was like twenty-five thousand! It was amazing. It meant independence. It meant that I could buy my mother some-thing. She was so great, so understanding, raising all of us kids after my dad died. I'll never forget the first thing I bought her. It was one of those fox wraps that bite their own tails. It was really wonderful to be able to give something back to my mom.

As much as it will be tempting to spend Broadway's comparatively large salary, save as much as you spend. No show runs forever, or if it does span decades like *Phantom of the Opera*, you might not choose to stay. This is not to say you must turn into a Scrooge. My memories of eve-nings out with members of the casts of *Drood*, *The Rink*, *The Grand Tour*, and so many more of the shows I worked on are far more precious than the few thousand dollars I could have saved. Not only was it a whooping good time, but I became friends with many of the principals I hardly saw during the show. But truthfully, money in the bank buys you security and independence in the iffy business of theatre.

ROBERT MONTANO: I believe in saving money. If you have capital behind you, you won't have to take jobs that you don't like doing. I did that with *Kiss of the Spider Woman*. I was making filthy money during the run and socked it away. I left *Spider Woman* after three years because I was offered the lead in a beautiful play at the Humana Festival at the Actors Theatre of Louisville. I made shit money during the run of the play, but I had enough in my bank to take that job and feed my soul to keep my creative juices aflow.

How Long to Stay in a Show

In some cases, you have no choice of how long to stay with one show. You open, the critics pummel the production, there's no advanced sale, and you close. The producers may try to hang in for a couple of months but it still feels like zip, zap, over, done, you're out of a job. Once the closing notice is posted, you receive one week's pay and that's it, baby. On the other hand, you may be in a mega-hit. As a newcomer to Broadway, I suggest you don't stay in the same show until you are too old to kick. Sure, you might be able to buy a condo, but one show is a mere petal in the flower of your career.

Let's say that you are in a production that will last a few years. Most likely you are on a six-month rider so you can't even entertain visions of leaving for another ensemble job within that time. Nor should you. The first six months to a year, depending on the season you opened, are filled with excitement. You appear on television talk shows, news programs, and the Macy's Thanksgiving Day Parade. The show cuts the cast album and may reshoot the television commercial, where you will not only gain a speck of immortality, but also your SAG and AFTRA cards. All sorts of benefits and televised specials clamor for numbers from the show and certain fashion magazines incorporate the cast in their layouts. In the spring you gear up for the Tony nominations and ultimately vie for the awards in June. All of these opportunities are a real gas and not to be missed. You've earned them.

From the business point of view, you are both a creative and financial investment. Through the entire rehearsal process, the choreographer and director molded their work around the cast's talents. You heard, digested, and experimented with their intents firsthand until the show developed into a complete physical production. To replace you means replacing a history, not just a slot. For better or worse, the show slips into a slightly different gear with each replacement. From a monetary point of view, the producers have invested in you and hope to maintain the original cast as long as possible. The show is the creative commodity the producers nurtured and presents to the audience each night. Besides that, each replacement means spending more money. While the new person is being trained, the original dancer is still in the show so there are two salaries to pay. Extra money goes toward rehearsal space, pianists, new shoes, playbill changes, and new costumes if the original costume can't be altered. For all concerned, your loyalty to the show, at least through the Tonys, is important and will be remembered when the next show rolls around.

On the other hand, there comes a time to leave the nest. So much of this decision depends on the atmosphere in the theatre, your enjoyment of the work, and your future prospects. Some casts are innately surly, regardless of the excellence of the work onstage, and some casts are dreams. Certain choreography feels hideous to perform, while another constantly feeds your spirit. Ticket sales may irrevocably drop causing the closing to loom on the horizon. How well you deal with these possibilities indicates when you should plunge back into the audition scene. If the show is going to close, find a new job as soon as possible, preferably timed to stay through the demise. (It is totally possible to rehearse the new show during the day and perform the old one at night for the last couple of weeks of the run.) If you abhor the entire show, leave when your six-month rider is up. If there are only certain sections of the show you can't stand, hang in there. My trick was to openly say, "I hate this," to a fellow dancer who had the same sentiment just before starting a deplorable number. Inevitably we would laugh and hit the number with the professional commitment it deserved.

GRACIELA DANIELE: There are professional actors and dancers who love going to the theatre every day, and there are others who think of it as a job. Most of the time I think that dancers are okay for about six months and then they start getting kind of tired. Doing the same thing eight performances a week tires the body and if someone doesn't have a big part, it is very hard to keep the newness of it. I personally wish, with some exceptions, that they didn't stay for more than six months. But most of all, I wish they went away when they are bored with the show so that I can put in new blood and new energy. Of course, with contracts and all that, I'm not in control of that decision.

As in any family, there are squabbles among the cast. This situation is tricky. Should you leave a show just because you can't stand the preshow and backstage life? No. Adjust your routine and adjust your attitude. Many times personalities flare over relatively nothing. These situations lose steam in time. But sometimes there are performers who are just plain unchangeable jerks. Rather than letting their antics fester in you, avoid them. If the dressing room drives you nuts, plan your makeup, dressing, and warm-up time for when the irritants aren't there, even if it means getting to the theatre earlier than usual. Wherever a boor reigns during offstage time, retreat to a different room, read a book, watch the show from the wings, or visit the people you like in the costume, hair, stage management, and tech departments. Find peace in your little world and no jerk will be able to tarnish the enjoyment of your job.

CHITA RIVERA: It's very important to enjoy the moment you are in and to enjoy the people around you. I seldom was in my dressing room, but in the wings watching. That's how I learned the tricks, the styles. And what happens from enjoying everybody is they give energy back to you. Just when you think you can't make it—that it's your last breath—look at the face of another dancer and they will give that breath back to you. Totally. The stage is a great playground to learn a lot.

When you artistically, emotionally, and physically feel antsy, and no vacation quells the urge to move on, plan your future. Audition for everything. Talk to the stage management about a viable time to give notice so you don't leave the show in a lurch. Save every penny to tide you over. For some dancers, the ideal situation is to land a show that goes into rehearsal a few weeks after their final performance. During the off time, they renew their energy, take class, heal injuries, and enjoy a Sunday brunch without having to run to their three o'clock matinees. Other dancers find diving into a new show more refreshing than a week in the country. Still others focus away from the Broadway scene and toward regional theatres to further their acting and singing careers. Just remember that the competition will always remain fierce and there are no guarantees you will get another job soon. Audition for the venues that interest you, and if an offer comes, take that next step on the road to your career. Each new show, each new person you meet, holds a surprise and will enhance your life and your love of the Broadway stage.

CHAPTER TWELVE

Final Advice and Fare Thee Well

You know how when you are making the rounds of good-byes at a party, multitudes of topics pop up that keep you there fifteen minutes more? So it is with this book. As I and all of the talented people interviewed in these pages wish you well, here are some final pieces of encouragement and advice.

MICHAEL KUBALA: Don't limit yourself. Go out and try everything your heart tells you because no one can say, "No," except you. If you are a little afraid, try not to be. You are going to come up against so many things in life that are just as difficult as getting to Broadway, if not more so, especially if your heart isn't in another profession. If dancing is your dream, know that it is your blessing.

MAMIE DUNCAN-GIBBS: Be willing to work hard. You can't sit back and say, "I'm not going to study this because it will take me five years to get good at it." Take the time. Get the proper training so you don't have to worry about not being good enough. If you fail temporarily, it doesn't make you a failure. It just means you failed in that circumstance. If it's in your heart to try again, figure it out. Okay, so you didn't make it one way—run around the block and try another door. I've run around so many blocks, I've seen the whole neighborhood.

LUIS PEREZ: Make sure you love to dance because it is too hard if you don't. And if you do love it, continue to learn about everything that is in your life. Some of the smartest people I've met are performers—smarter than doctors and lawyers. The best performers use the amount of knowledge they have about politics, science, the whole world. This knowledge goes hand in hand with our profession because we create new worlds.

GRACIELA DANIELE: Practice, practice, practice. Train your bodies. And work your mind as well as your bodies. By that I mean read, listen to music, look at art—get cultured. A school education is not enough. You must always expand your mind.

CAITLIN CARTER: Some people have the opinion that if you are really serious about dance, you don't go to college. Sometimes I think that if I had it to do over I would've skipped college and come to New York earlier. On the other hand, I don't regret it. I got an amazing education that I may use someday if I stop dancing. My advice is to study hard so that you are as prepared as possible. New York is great, but it's tough.

DAVID WARREN-GIBSON: You have to learn to love the roller coaster. The down times are going to be as low as the up times are going to be high. You can't have one without the other. You have to get used to that and learn to love it, because that's part of what show business is. If you follow your dream, you can't go wrong with the ups and downs. If you feel it inside of you, you've got to do it. Otherwise, your life is like death.

CHITA RIVERA: I deeply believe that you need a sense of humor to really make it in dance. Don't take yourself so seriously. Have a sense of humor because a sense of humor will get you through everything. It will also make you friends.

JULIO MONGE: Don't get stuck on the idea of the higher leg or better arch, but remember that dancing on Broadway is an art that encompasses your acting, your voice, your whole persona. It is your input as an artist that raises theatrical dance to a higher creative level, and it is your responsibility to look within yourself to see if you are willing to work hard on your craft to make an honest contribution. If you are inspired and happy, you will tap into a part of you that is true, and that truth is the most important thing to hold onto at the end of the day.

JOANN M. HUNTER: One girl might come to New York and snap, book a job; another might wait two years. It's just how it is. There are very few jobs and so many people who vie for those jobs. And New York is expensive—you've got to deal with that. But if you really love it, have a passion for it, you will find a way.

EUGENE FLEMING: There are people who try something, can't get it, and don't want to try again. Dance isn't immediate. The beauty is in the trying, the challenge to go from move to move, class to class, show to show. I feel blessed that I have been able to be here on Broadway. To do some work. And also for me to learn because I'm still perfecting the craft of performing. I like to think I know something, but I don't know anything when it comes down to it. Every time I get out there onstage I'm a beginner, but I trust the instincts of the groundwork that I've laid.

BEBE NEUWIRTH: Behave yourself. Be courteous. Be professional. Respect your fellow performers and the building—the theatre. This isn't just "showbiz." Within that sacred building, what we are doing is creative and artistic. Proper behavior is always appreciated by the people you work with. If for no other reason, do it so you can get hired again.

ROBERT MONTANO: Don't be so busy or self-involved that you don't listen to older people. They have something to share that captures the nuances of life that you could put into your own life, as well as your work. If you don't know how to listen, how are you ever going to learn?

TOMMY TUNE: I wish I had documented my life. I wish I had come home from an audition that I either got or didn't get, or the important day I finally did a double tour, and wrote my feelings down at that moment. A life worth living is a life worth documenting. And every day in the life of a dancer—every accomplishment—is so important. Because dance is evanescent in that it only exists in time and space at that moment—now you see it, now you don't. It's not anything like a song or a painting that you did. It's into thin air. That's what makes it so fabulous. That's its value. And you have to know that you gave it—that you made it happen. It's a lot. It's a fine thing.

JIM BORSTELMANN: Ask yourself what's more important: living your life through other people's ideas of what you should do or following your dream? Those people are not going to be with you through your whole life. Buddies will grow up and be gone. They won't matter. Follow your own dream. You have to. You're going to love it.

Experience, determination, and risk are the bywords to grow into a true professional on Broadway. And what an exciting venture it is! Creating theatre is such a limitless arena, all of us who work on Broadway amiably envy each other because we can't do it all. For every show we perform, we want to experience what another dancer is learning in the theatre next door. And that envy now passes on to you, to the opportunities you have in store, to the creative, dedicated, passionate, hilarious people you will meet, and even to the struggle of paying the rent. I wouldn't trade the thrills, the sweat, and the disappointments for anything, anywhere. It's living life to the fullest. It's dancing a dream come true. It's Broadway. I hope to see you there soon.

The Cast of Contributors

Added together, the fourteen people I interviewed for this book, plus myself, have worked on a total of 167 Broadway shows and national tours as performers, directors, and choreographers. This does not include the hundreds of Off-Broadway and regional shows, television, film, nightclub acts, and stage revues for which many of the contributors are well known. Listed below are strictly the Broadway shows and tours. As of this printing, the list keeps growing!

Jim Borstelmann: *Jerome Robbins' Broadway; Damn Yankees; Chicago; The Producers.* (Photograph by Craig Sugimoto)

Caitlin Carter: *Ain't Broadway Grand; Victor, Victoria; Crazy For You; My Fair Lady; Mame; Chicago; A Chorus Line; Swing; Bells Are Ringing.* (Photograph by Arthur L. Cohen)

Graciela Daniele: *What Makes Sammy Run; Here's Where I Belong; Promises, Promises; CoCo; Chicago (1975); Follies. Choreography: History of American Film; The Most Happy Fella; The Pirates of Penzance; Zorba; The Rink; The Mystery of Edwin Drood; The Goodbye Girl; Ragtime. Direction and choreography: Dangerous Games; Once on This Island; Chronicle of a Death Foretold; Marie Christine; Annie Get Your Gun.*

Mamie Duncan-Gibbs: *Dangerous Games; Joseph and the Amazing Technicolor Dreamcoat; Cats; Sweet Charity; Damn Yankees; Jelly's Last Jam; Chicago; Kiss Me, Kate; The Boys from Syracuse.*
(Photograph by Ron Rinaldi)

Eugene Fleming: *A Chorus Line; Sophisticated Ladies; The Tap Dance Kid; The Wiz; Song and Dance; Black and Blue; High Rollers Social and Pleasure Club; Swingin' on a Star; Smokey Joe's Café; Street Corner Symphony; One Mo' Time; Fosse; Kiss Me, Kate; Dream Girls; Look of Love.* (Photograph by James K. Kriegsmann Jr.)

David Warren-Gibson: *A Chorus Line; Dancin'; Dreamgirls; Sweet Charity; Chicago.* (Photograph by Andrew Brucker)

JoAnn M. Hunter: *West Side Story; Cats; Chicago; Jerome Robbins' Broadway; Shogun, the Musical; Miss Saigon; Guys and Dolls; Damn Yankees; How to Succeed in Business Without Really Trying; A Funny Thing Happened on the Way to the Forum; Steel Pier; Kiss Me, Kate; Thou Shalt Not; Thoroughly Modern Millie.* (Photograph by Alan Ariano)

Michael Kubala: *A Broadway Musical; Marilyn, An American Fable; Dancin'; Woman of the Year; On Your Toes; Pippin; Jerome Robbins' Broadway; Crazy for You; Chicago.* (Photograph by David Cross)

Julio Monge: *Jerome Robbins' Broadway; Twelfth Night; Chronicle of a Death Foretold; Victor, Victoria; The Capeman; Fosse.* (Photograph by Tim Schultheis)

Robert Montano: *West Side Story; Kiss of the Spider Woman; Cats; Legs Diamond; On the Town.* (Photograph by Brad Calcaterra)

Bebe Neuwirth: *A Chorus Line; Little Me; Dancin'; Sweet Charity; Damn Yankees; Chicago; Fosse.* (Photograph by Michael Lamont)

Luis Perez: *West Side Story; Phantom of the Opera; Jerome Robbins' Broadway; Dangerous Games; Grand Hotel; Man of La Mancha* (1992); *Ain't Broadway Grand; Chronicle of a Death Foretold; Passion; Chicago. Choreography: The Civil War; Man of La Mancha* (2002). Fight Direction: *Dangerous Games; Wild Party; Marie Christine; Man of La Mancha* (2002).
(Photograph by James K. Kriegsmann Jr.)

Chita Rivera: *Call Me Madam; Guys and Dolls; Can-Can; Seventh Heaven; Mr. Wonderful; West Side Story; Bye Bye Birdie; The Threepenny Opera; Sweet Charity; Born Yesterday; The Rose Tattoo; Zorba; Kiss Me, Kate; Chicago* (1975); *Bring Back Birdie; Merlin; The Rink; Jerry's Girls; Kiss of the Spider Woman; Chicago* (1999); *Nine.*
(Photograph by Joan Marcus)

Tommy Tune: *Irma La Douce; Baker Street; A Joyful Noise; How Now Dow Jones; See Saw; Bye Bye Birdie; My One and Only; Tommy Tune Tonight; Busker Alley.* Direction and choreography: *The Best Little Whorehouse in Texas; A Day in Hollywood, A Night in the Ukraine; Nine; My One and Only; Grand Hotel; The Will Rogers Follies; The Best Little Whorehouse Goes Public.*
(Photograph by Franco LaCosta)